RIDE GUIDE

North Jersey

2nd Edition
By Dan Goldfischer

New Off-Road Section
By Ellen R. Otto

White Meadow Press

Ride Guide North Jersey
Second Edition (1996 Revision)
Copyright 1994 by Daniel Goldfischer

Cover: photo, Sunrise Mountain Road by Daniel Goldfischer; design by Karen Strattner.

Illustrations: Kathy Murray-Allison, page 10 (poison ivy), page 50 (Tempe Wick House), page 64 (turtle), page 116 (Peter's Valley Store). Karen Strattner, page 16 (monument at Montclair's Memorial Park), page 18 (Cathedral of the Sacred Heart, Newark), page 48 (Ringwood Manor), page 76 (fence at Morristown National Historic Park), page 84 (Lake Marcia and High Point Monument), page 94 (Keen's Mill), page 109 (rural Sussex scene), page 118 (Delaware Water Gap), page 129 (Blairstown), page 135 (River Road), page 146 (Little Falls path), page 152 (log and bike), page 153 (Patriot's Path sign), page 168 (Sussex Branch trail sign).

Maps: Gayle Rembold-Furbert, Dan Goldfischer, Sabine Peifer.

ISBN 0-933855-08-7
Library of Congress Catalog Card Number: 94-60243

Also available
Bed, Breakfast & Bike New England
Bed, Breakfast & Bike Mid-Atlantic
Bed, Breakfast & Bike Northern California
Bed, Breakfast & Bike Pacific Northwest
Ride Guide Hudson Valley and Sound Shore
Ride Guide Central Jersey

Send for our catalog:
Anacus Press, Inc.
P.O. Box 4544
Warren, NJ 07059

Published by
WHITE MEADOW PRESS
a Division of

P. O. Box 4544, Warren, New Jersey 07059

"Ride Guide" and "Bed Breakfast & Bike" are trademarks of Anacus Press, Inc.

Printed in the United States of America

To Shar, forever my Shining Star;
and to Eric, our Rising Star

CONTENTS

PREFACE

In 1985, the original incarnation of this book, *RIDE GUIDE For North Jersey and Beyond,* first appeared. Four years later, White Meadow Press, responding to the book's popularity and the growth of cycling in New Jersey, split the original volume into two books: *RIDE GUIDE/North Jersey* and *RIDE GUIDE/Central Jersey.* These editions reflected the continued urbanization and suburbanization of the state, with changed route starting points. It also helped cyclists find attractive routes in the older suburban areas of Essex and Bergen counties.

This second edition of *RIDE GUIDE/North Jersey* features a brand new section on the best off-road bike riding in the region, written by Ellen R. Otto, an experienced mountain bike rider and leader of off-road rides for the Morris Area Freewheelers. We've done our best to incorporate our usual cue sheet system in rides where landmarks may be trees and bushes—a cycle computer and a trail map would be most useful accessories.

For road rides, this edition features several brand-new rides in Warren and Sussex Counties, and revisions of existing routes where conditions have changed over four years. The routes that are carried over from earlier *RIDE GUIDE*s are still beautiful, interesting and fun.

For riders new to *RIDE GUIDE*, here are remarks from last edition's preface that describe the joy of cycling in North Jersey:

Cycle-touring amidst the quiet roads of old planned suburbs and urban parks is quite enjoyable because there are a wealth of cultural treasures to see along the way, such as iris gardens, the lab and home of our most famous inventor and one of the largest cathedrals in the world (on the **Montclair-Branch Brook Park** route) and the manor of a 19th century iron lord (on the **Ringwood-West Milford** route).

Of course we have not neglected rides through farmland and along bucolic streams. Using our easy-to-read maps, you can enjoy miles of quiet roads along the Delaware River on new routes that take you from Port Jervis to Dingman's Ferry, south to the Delaware Water Gap, and from Belvidere to the Pohatcong Creek. Sussex County, reminiscent of New England with its many dairy farms, gets thorough coverage.

For those of you new to cycling, or new to riding in New Jersey, here is just a sample of what you're going to experience taking a mini-vacation on two wheels, taken from the imaginary "diary of a cyclist":

"Driving out to Belvidere, about 45 minutes west of busy Parsippany (formerly a chicken-farming town that now grows office parks and hotels), I am struck by how rural some parts of New Jersey still are. I grab a snack from the A&P at the start of the route and set off.

"Belvidere is the Warren County seat but is so quiet. I guess gentrification hasn't hit here yet. Immediately the route goes downhill to the Delaware River. What a beautiful road! Narrow, totally free of traffic, it's what I picture European roads to be like, not those of the most densely populated state. There are a couple of hills to challenge me, but nothing my 12-speed can't handle.

"Phillipsburg is the only busy spot along the way, but drivers are courteous to cyclists. Soon I am breaking out my picnic lunch alongside Pohatcong Creek, enjoying the shade of the trees and the sound of the brook.

"On the way back I pass an 18th Century stone grist mill and a number of farmhouses dating to the same period. There are lots of good pictures to take—the kind you hang on your office wall to remind you of weekend bike rides!

"There is a short climb to the top of Ridge Road, and the reward is a commanding view all the way to the Delaware Water Gap. Hawks circle overhead, rising on the thermals and calling to each other. A nearby wild raspberry bush invites an impromptu snack.

"I am back in Belvidere before I knew it. Another great ride."

Welcome to New Jersey cycling, and welcome to the second edition of *RIDE GUIDE/North Jersey*!

BEFORE YOU GO

The beauty of cycling is that it is a simple sport. You don't have to worry that much about equipment, not compared to a sport like boating or scuba diving. And thanks to *RIDE GUIDE,* you don't have to travel far to enjoy good routes.

But there are certain things that will make your bike tour more enjoyable. Check the weather report and dress accordingly: If it's below 60 degrees when you start off, most sports medicine experts recommend wearing long sweatpants or tights. As it warms up, change into shorts (or peel off your tights you wore over your bike shorts). It might be a good idea to pack a rain jacket in a handlebar or rack-top bag just in case. Ponchos and cycling don't mix, due to the possibility of chain or wheel entanglement.

Speaking of keeping things out of the chain, riders who don't wear tights might take a few hints from old-timers and use trouser clips to prevent flapping or greasy pant legs. Also, double-knot your shoelaces and tuck them into your shoes—we've seen a few crashes due to excess lace length reaching the front changer or getting caught between the chain and chainwheel.

Be sure to bring plenty of water. Sip from your bottle every 10 minutes or so, because cycling takes quite a bit of fluid out of you, even when it's cool out. Also, take along snacks. Most of our routes have deli stops, but some may not be for the first 20 miles, so you might want to be prepared for early hunger pangs with some fruit, gorp or cookies.

Basic tools such as tire irons, frame pump, patch kit, screw driver, Allen wrenches and the like (and knowledge of how to use them) are necessary for the well-prepared cyclist. Most local bike clubs and many bike stores hold clinics on repairing flat tires, adjusting derailleurs, fixing broken cables and taking care of other things that might go wrong on the road. May you never have to use this knowledge, but it's always good to have, just in case.

On certain routes, carrying insect repellent is a good idea. This is especially true when travelling on dirt roads between June and September, or if the lunch spot is a woodsy park. Also, watch out for poison ivy. That pleasant-looking three-leaved vine climbing the tree on which your bike is leaning may give you a rash later. It grows in profusion on roads bordering farm fields.

Finally you should not ride without your life insurance—a hard-shelled, ANSI-approved, Snell-rated helmet. There have been a number of instances in the last few years where this simple item has made the difference between a crashing rider becoming a vegetable, or a statistic, or remaining around to cycle many more New Jersey roads in good health. The newest helmets are made of incredibly lightweight polystyrene, and you don't even realize you have it on. Invest in a helmet and then use it!

Mountain bike riders, see the introduction to the off-road section for special hints on riding mountain and hybrid bikes on trails.

Have a happy, safe tour and thanks for using *RIDE GUIDE*.

HOW TO USE THIS BOOK

RIDE GUIDE/North Jersey is organized into four sections according to the county where the route starts, and a fifth section covering off-road routes throughout the region. As a general rule in Northern New Jersey, the further west you go, the less traffic you'll encounter and the more rural the ride will be.

The route title generally contains the origin point and an important destination along the way. All routes are loops and return to their starting points. Some include optional extra mileage, and a few include instructions to combine routes for more ambitious riders.

Mileage is only one factor in determining which route to follow, but it's an important one. If you've never cycle-toured before, it is probably best to start with a mileage under 30. Don't let these numbers intimidate you! Even beginners can tool along at 12 mph or better on flat roads. And if you have the whole day or even half a day, you won't have to hurry to finish a 30-mile ride.

Other factors to consider are listed under each ride. They are **terrain, traffic, road conditions**, and **points of interest**.

Terrain is probably the most important element in your choice of a ride. New Jersey, especially North Jersey, is not flat. We've gone out of our way to avoid climbing mountain ranges (yes, we do have the Appalachians, Kittatinnies, Watchungs, and various Long Hill Roads). But there will be ascents and descents. A "gently rolling" ride might strike the novice as hilly and the advanced rider as "no sweat." You will find yourself building "hill endurance" (and leg muscles) as you do these rides, and becoming more comfortable with that upturn in terrain ahead.

Traffic is an important consideration, especially when riding on a weekday. A "moderate" road may get a little busier around 5 pm on a Friday. *RIDE GUIDE* routes avoid the busy roads as much as possible. If you like routes that feature more cows than cars, look for traffic descriptions of "light", "extra light" and "positively sleepy."

Road Conditions vary greatly around New Jersey, and often even within the small area covered by a bike route. Unfortunately, with all the growth and construction around the state even many back roads suffer choppy and bumpy pavement (from sewer line digs and the like), and this is noted in the write-up for each route. If there are dirt roads, they will be noted here as well. Dirt roads quite often are the most scenic and quiet, so we do not avoid them in this book.

Points of Interest tells where to get off your bike, whip out your camera, notebook, or sketchpad, spread a picnic towel (not too many cyclists carry blankets!), jump in for a swim, fill your water bottle, or stop for ice cream. Sometimes there are no specific buildings to tour or shops to see and the listing under this category will be "quiet, pretty back roads." This means you are sure to encounter beautiful spots along the way for photographing or just relaxing. That's what makes cycle-touring such a great activity!

Directions to Starting Point tell you how to reach the beginning of the route by car. If you wish to go by public transportation, better have someone else bring your bike: when this book was published, New Jersey Transit still didn't allow bicycles on its buses and trains.

Cue sheets tell you every turn and point of interest along the way. Read them one line ahead and you'll be able to spot the next turn. On the cue sheets, **Pt.-Pt.** indicates the mileage from the last turn or point of interest. **Cume**, short for cumulative, lists total mileage from the starting point. The abbreviations in the **Direction** column are:

B	Left
R	Right
S	Straight
BL	Bear Left
BR	Bear Right

SL   Sharp Left
SR   Sharp Right

In the **streets/landmarks** column, only the street you are going to be on is printed in **boldface**. Watch for cautions and other warnings listed in this column pertaining to steep hills, trafficky roads, hard to find turns, etc. A (T) is where the road ends in another road, and you must go either right or left.

Maps will help you navigate the main route as well as find shortcuts back to the starting point should you need them. If you are on a road for a long time and are not sure whether you're on the right road, turn to the map: there may be landmarks and cross streets listed on the map that were not noted on the cue sheet.

The maps include markings to indicate hills, dirt roads and busy streets. It is still a good idea to include a local street map in your bike bag along with *RIDE GUIDE*. Road configurations can change with construction of developments, and occasionally street signs disappear or are turned around.

RIDE STARTING POINTS MAP

Use the map on page 15 to help you locate the starting points of all routes described in *RIDE GUIDE/North Jersey*. The triangles indicate off-road routes.

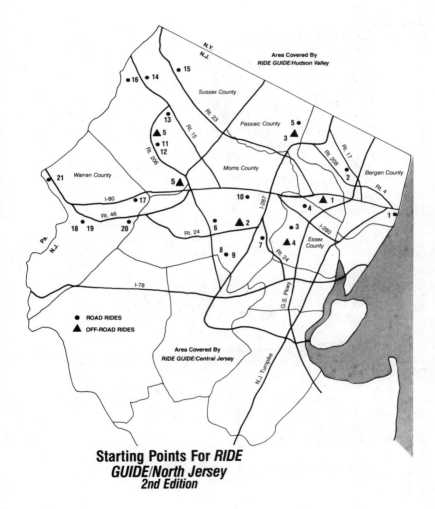

Starting Points For *RIDE GUIDE/North Jersey*
2nd Edition

RIDES STARTING IN BERGEN, PASSAIC, AND ESSEX COUNTIES

The northeastern corner of New Jersey is not generally thought of as prime cycling country because it is the state's urban core. Besides the big, congested old cities, there are long-developed suburban tracts with shopping centers and busy highways with office parks and still more busy highways. And yet...

Mixed up in this congested concentration of cars and people are some incredibly pretty parks, quiet suburban roads, wealthy estates, unusual views, the Hudson River, reservoirs and lakes, and some important historical attractions. The beauty of riding in these counties is the rides are very close to home for many *RIDE GUIDE* readers.

Ft. Lee-Nyack features the Palisades, a wilderness area just outside New York City. Enjoy cycling inside Palisades Interstate Park on a car-free road halfway down the cliffs. Head up the Hudson River to the pretty New York State communities of Piermont and Nyack, with their antique shops and quaint atmospheres. Then ride on a bike path on the shores of the river under the cliff. Climb a hill to Rockland Lake State Park, then head back south on quiet suburban roads.

Northern Bergen County explores still-quiet areas near the New York State border. Ride north from Ho-Ho-Kus to Mahwah and spend some time at Darlington Park and Ramapo Valley Reservation before heading south through Ramsey, Allendale and Waldwick.

Livingston-Watchung Reservation spins around the foothills of the Watchung Mountains, visiting two arboretums and a major park with a good science museum. This route passes the large mansions of Short Hills. It's a good beginner ride and an excellent "quick workout" for more experienced cyclists.

Montclair-Branch Brook Park loops through the old, gracious suburban towns surrounding Newark. There are some interesting places to visit along these tree-lined, gas-lit roads, including the Edison National Historic Site, Montclair Art Museum and Presby Memorial Iris Gardens. The ride's destination is Branch Brook Park, home in April of the East Coast's most beautiful cherry blossom display (Washington D.C., eat your heart out!). And that huge cathedral reflected in the park's lake is the Cathedral of the Sacred Heart, one of the world's largest.

For a loop in northern Passaic County, try **Ringwood-West Milford.** This ride pokes around the hills and valleys surrounding Wanaque Reservoir and the Newark Watershed and includes the relaxingly quiet and beautiful nine-mile Clinton Road. An extra loop at the end covers Ringwood State Park, with its historic mansions, botanical gardens, and lake beach.

FT. LEE-NYACK—47.8 MILES

This ride is the most accessible New Jersey bike route for cyclists living in New York City, who can ride over the George Washington Bridge to the start of the route. Riders who are used to western New Jersey cycling are surprised at the amazing quiet beauty of the Palisades, so close to the big city yet as wild and "woodsy" as places 80 miles away.

Terrain: Flat to gently rolling while paralleling the river. Expect some strenuous climbs and fast descents when travelling east or west.

Traffic: Moderate, for the most part. Beautiful Henry Hudson Drive is reserved for bikes.

Road Conditions: Very smooth, generally, with some bumpy sections.

Points of Interest: Fort Lee Historic Park (visitor's center, interpretive trails, and great views of Manhattan); riding through **Palisades Interstate Park**, **Tallman Mountain** and **Rockland Lake State Parks** (**swimming pools** in the latter two parks—use a sturdy lock if leaving your bike at the pool); **Piermont Pier**; the antiquing town of **Nyack**; bike path on the river at **Nyack State Park**; **George Washington Bridge** bike path.

The Hudson River forms the northeastern border of New Jersey, and while many New Jerseyans associate the riverbank with dilapidated piers surrounded by high-rise condos, north of Edgewater the entire riverfront is within Palisades Interstate Park. This park is one of the most beautiful and dramatic stretches of green in the state.

Thanks to the efforts of New Jersey's bicycle clubs, a 4-mile stretch of Henry Hudson Drive is open only to bikes. This road takes you through the ancient tree cover under the cliffs, with fantastic views of river and the city across the river. The climb back up the Palisades is exhilarating, to say the least!

Note that in adverse weather conditions and in the winter, park police may close the road to bikes. Please obey signs.

North of Alpine, ride on Route 9W, which has a wide shoulder and little traffic. After crossing into New York State, cycle through Tallman Mountain Park. The park has a relatively uncrowded swimming pool (compared to the one at Rockland Lake State Park), and the admission fee is reasonable.

The road from Piermont to Nyack, very popular with cyclists from New York City, contains some houses with unusual architecture and great river views. You might wish to take a short detour in Piermont and ride out on the pier that gives the town its name. It extends over a mile into the river and has a great view of the Tappan Zee Bridge. World War I troops boarded ships here that carried them to Europe.

Nyack has many interesting antique stores and good restaurants. North of Nyack, the route takes you down Broadway, with huge mansions facing the river. Pedal under Hook Mountain on the 2.5-mile riverfront bike path in Nyack State Park. Then climb to Rockland Lake, a nice place for a picnic except on summer weekends when it is very crowded.

The return route to Fort Lee takes you over quiet suburban roads that are mostly flat. The climb up the Palisades is achieved on a winding series of pretty residential streets in Englewood, somewhat minimizing the pain.

Just before you return to Fort Lee Historic Park, you might wish to pedal over the George Washington Bridge for more dramatic views of city and river.

Directions to Starting Point: Fort Lee Historic Park is on Hudson Terrace in Fort Lee. From New Jersey, approach the George Washington Bridge on the local lanes of I-95 and take the last right-hand exit before the toll booths, marked "Fort Lee." Continue straight ahead parallel to the highway for several traffic lights until you reach Hudson Terrace. Turn right and the park entrance is on the left almost immediately. There is a small fee for parking.

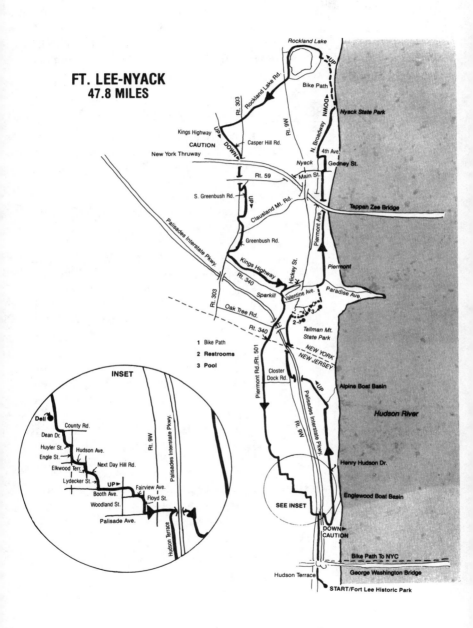

FT. LEE-NYACK
47.8 MILES

Rockland Lake

Rt. 303

Rockland Lake Rd.

Bike Path

Rt. 9W

UP

DOWN

Nyack State Park

Kings Highway

CAUTION

New York Thruway

UP

DOWN

Casper Hill Rd.

N. Broadway

4th Ave.

Nyack

Gedney St.

Rt. 59

Main St.

S. Greenbush Rd.

UP

Clausland Mt. Rd.

Tappan Zee Bridge

Palisades Interstate Pkwy.

Greenbush Rd.

Piermont Ave.

Kings Highway

Rt. 340

Hickey St.

Piermont

Rt. 303

Sparkill

Valentine Ave.

Paradise Ave.

Oak Tree Rd.

Rt. 340

3

2

Tallman Mt.
State Park

Piermont Rd./Rt. 501

NEW YORK
NEW JERSEY

1 Bike Path

2 **Restrooms**

3 Pool

Closter
Dock Rd.

UP

Alpine Boat Basin

Palisades Interstate Pkwy.

Rt. 9W

Hudson River

INSET

Dell

County Rd.

Dean Dr.

Huyler St.

Hudson Ave.

Engle St.

Elkwood Terr.

Next Day Hill Rd.

Lydecker St.

UP

Fairview Ave.

Booth Ave.

Floyd St.

Woodland St.

Palisade Ave.

Rt. 9W

Palisades Interstate Pkwy.

Hudson Terrace

Henry Hudson Dr.

Englewood Boat Basin

SEE INSET

DOWN
CAUTION

Bike Path To NYC

Hudson Terrace

George Washington Bridge

START/Fort Lee Historic Park

From New York City, there is an exit from the upper level of the George Washington Bridge for Hudson Terrace. Turn right at the bottom of the ramp, and the park is on the left in 0.2 miles. Cyclists from New York can come over on the George Washington Bridge bike path, which ends on Hudson Terrace north of the park.

PT.-PT.	CUME	DIRECTION	STREET/LANDMARK
0.0	0.0		Exit Fort Lee Historic Park parking lot down the entrance road
0.1	0.1	**R**	**Hudson Terrace** (T)
2.0	2.1	**R**	**Palisade Ave.** (T) NOTE: If the park road is marked "closed", you must turn **left** here, then turn **right** in 0.1 miles onto **Sylvan Ave./Rt. 9W**, and rejoin the main cue sheet at Mile 8.5. You might wish to turn right first and enjoy a river view at the top of the road leading down to the park before heading back to Rt. 9W. *Use EXTREME CAUTION heading down the steep, winding road into the park.*
0.5	2.6	**BL**	At fork onto **Henry Hudson Dr.** Do not head down to Englewood Boat Basin
4.4	7.0	**BL**	Toward Rt. 9W at fork. Do not head down to Alpine Boat Basin
1.5	8.5	**R**	**Rt. W North** (traffic light)
2.9	11.4		Entering New York State
1.1	12.5	**R**	Onto **bike path** (just past "Indian Motorcycle" sign on right)
1.4	13.9		Restrooms on right
0.3	14.2	**R**	At end of bike path (T)
0.1	14.3	**R**	At T; follow **bike route** signs

PT.-PT.	CUME	DIRECTION	STREET/LANDMARK
0.2	14.5	**R**	At traffic circle toward **pool** (following bike route signs)
0.1	14.6	**L**	To continue on **bike path.** (Turn sharp right if you wish to stop at Tallman Mountain **pool**)
0.5	15.1	**R**	At end of path. Cross steel deck bridge onto **Piermont Ave.**
0.1	15.2		Turn right onto **Paradise Ave.** for side trip to Piermont Pier (about 2 miles round trip) A **deli** is on the right shortly after this intersection (on the Main St. of Piermont)
3.7	18.9	**R**	**Main St.**, Nyack (T)
0.0	18.9	**L**	First left onto **Gedney St.**
0.2	19.1	**L**	**4th Avenue**
0.2	19.3	**R**	**North Broadway** (stop sign; no street sign)
1.7	21.0	**R**	Into **Nyack State Park.** Go down the hill. (Restrooms and water on left at bottom of hill)
0.3	21.3	**S**	Onto **bike route** next to river
1.3	22.6	**BL**	At bike path fork
0.2	22.8		Emerge from bike path and climb steep hill
0.4	23.2	**R**	At fork (no sign) just past firehouse. **Rockland Lake State Park** (with a swimming pool) will be on your left
1.0	24.2	**S**	At first exit for Rt. 9W to continue circling lake
1.2	25.4	**BR**	At second exit for Rt. 9W
0.1	25.5	**S**	Cross Rt. 9W at stop sign onto **Rockland Lake Rd.**
1.3	26.8	**S**	Cross Rt. 303 at traffic light

PT.-PT.	CUME	DIRECTION	STREET/LANDMARK
0.4	27.2	**L**	**Kings Highway** (T)
0.6	27.8	**S**	At stop sign. Road becomes **Casper Hill Rd.**
0.4	28.2	**BR**	Onto **Rt. 303.** *CAUTION: Very steep downhill before this intersection. Control your speed!*
0.9	29.1	**L**	After Rt. 59 underpass. Walk bike, as there is a no left turn sign here
0.2	29.3	**R**	**South Greenbush Rd.,** toward Rockland Center for the Arts
1.2	30.5	**S**	At stop sign. Road becomes **Greenbush Rd. North**
0.5	31.0	**L**	**Rt. 303 South** (T)
0.2	31.2	**BL**	**Greenbush Rd.** Use caution crossing Rt. 303, a busy road
0.7	31.9	**S**	At stop sign, crossing Clausland Mountain Rd.
0.6	32.5	**R**	Toward Rt. 303
0.1	32.6	**L**	**Rt. 303 South** (traffic light)
0.2	32.8	**L**	**Kings Highway** (Chemical Bank on corner; turn is before the traffic light; use caution!)
1.5	34.3	**BR**	At yield sign onto unmarked **Hickey St.**
0.1	34.4	**L**	Onto unmarked **Rt. 340** (T)
0.1	34.5	**S**	At traffic light with railroad running across middle of intersection
0.1	34.6	**R**	**Valentine Ave.**
0.1	34.7	**S**	At stop sign, to continue on **Rt. 340.** Union Ave. goes right
0.1	34.8	**BR**	To continue on **Rt. 340.** Note enormous 200-plus-year-old tree in front of restaurant on corner
1.5	36.3		Entering New Jersey. Road is now called **Piermont Rd.**

PT.-PT.	CUME	DIRECTION	STREET/LANDMARK
3.5	39.8	S	Cross Closter Dock Rd.
0.2	40.0		**Deli** on right
0.6	40.6	L	Curve left onto **County Rd./Rt. 501**
0.1	40.7	R	**Dean Dr./Rt. 501**
0.1	40.8	BL	At fork to continue on **Rt. 501/ Huyler St.** Road will change name to **Westervelt Ave.**
1.4	42.2	R	**Engle St./Rt. 501** (T)
0.6	42.8	L	**Hudson Ave.** (traffic light). Rt. 501 goes right
0.3	43.1	R	**Elkwood Terr.** (T)
0.1	43.2	L	**Lydecker St.**
0.1	43.3	R	Curve right to continue on **Lydecker St.** Next Day Hill Rd. goes left
0.2	43.5	S	Cross Glenwood St. at stop sign to continue on **Lydecker St.** (slight left jog)
0.2	43.7	L	**Booth Ave.** (stop sign)
0.6	44.3	S	Cross Woodland St. at stop sign
0.2	44.5	L	**Fairview Ave.** (T)
0.3	44.8	R	**Floyd St.** (T)
0.6	45.4	L	**Palisade Ave.** (stop sign)
0.2	45.6	R	**Hudson Terrace**
2.1	47.7	L	Into **Fort Lee Historic Park**
0.1	47.8		**Visitor's Center.** End of route

NORTHERN BERGEN COUNTY—24.3 MILES

Bergen County is one of those fully-developed suburban areas with plenty of quiet scenic roads that are likely to stay that way. RIDE GUIDE helps you find the scenery amidst the hustle and bustle. Here is an excellent beginner ride over lightly travelled roads in Northern Bergen.

Terrain: Very, very gentle. A few climbs and drops, but otherwise the contours will not wear out your shift levers.
Traffic: Moderate to occasionally busy. Except during rush hours, drivers seem to be considerate of cyclists.
Road Conditions: Choppy, bumpy pavement at times, especially on the busier roads where they seem to be forever installing new sewer or gas lines.
Points of Interest: Elmer's (a genuine country store); **Darlington Park** (swimming, picnicking); **Ramapo Valley Reservation** (picnicking, hiking); pleasant suburban and semi-rural roads of Northern Bergen County.

The quieter roads of Northern Bergen are the setting for this short loop that is a perfect ride for novices, a tone-up ride for more experienced riders who haven't been on the bike for awhile, and a good after-work ride for those warm summer evenings.

Start by heading north out of Ho-Ho-Kus. You will be in the flat, pretty valley of the Saddle River and go through towns named after it, including Upper Saddle River, the current home of former President Nixon. Elmer's Store is a real country general store in the midst of the wealthy suburbs. Inside are photos of patrons clad in Elmer's T-shirts standing in front of a variety of famous locations around the world.

Turn west on various roads paralleling the border with New York State. Because the hills go north to south, you will be experiencing some elevation change, but nothing a good multi-speed bike can't handle.

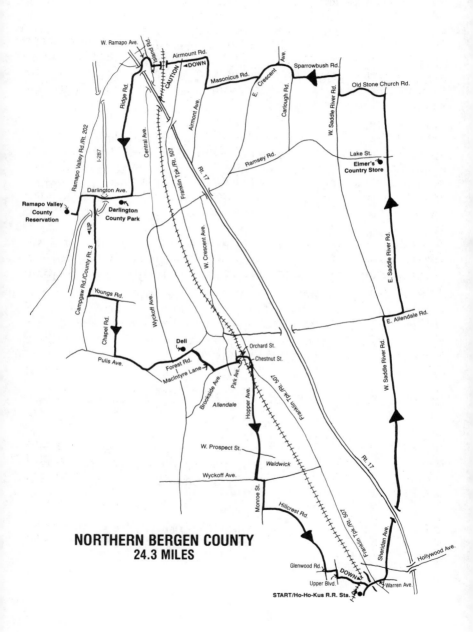

W. Ramapo Ave.

Island Rd.

Airmount Rd.

◄DOWN

Masonicus Rd.

E. Crescent Ave.

Sparrowbush Rd.

Old Stone Church Rd.

Ridge Rd.

CAUTION

Airmount Ave.

Carlough Rd.

W. Saddle River Rd.

Central Ave.

Ramapo Valley Rd./Rt. 202

I-287

Franklin Tpk./Rt. 507

Rt. 17

Ramsey Rd.

Lake St.

Elmer's Country Store

Darlington Ave.

Ramapo Valley County Reservation

Darlington County Park

E. Saddle River Rd.

▼UP

Campgaw Rd./County Rt. 3

W. Crescent Ave.

Youngs Rd.

Wyckoff Ave.

E. Allendale Rd.

Chapel Rd.

Deli

Orchard St.

Chestnut St.

W. Saddle River Rd.

Pulis Ave.

Forest Rd.

MacIntyre Lane

Brookside Ave.

Park Ave.

Hopper Ave.

Franklin Tpk./Rt. 507

Allendale

W. Prospect St.

Waldwick

Wyckoff Ave.

Monroe St.

Rt. 17

Sheridan Ave.

NORTHERN BERGEN COUNTY
24.3 MILES

Hillcrest Rd.

Franklin Tpk./Rt. 507

Hollywood Ave.

Glenwood Rd.

◄DOWN►

Warren Ave.

Upper Blvd.

START/Ho-Ho-Kus R.R. Sta.

In Mahwah you will come to the halfway point, a large area of parkland owned by Bergen County. Darlington Park has a swimming lake, but admission fees are quite steep for non-Bergen residents. Ramapo Valley Reservation has shady picnic areas along the Ramapo River and a pond, and the energetic can take a 30-minute hike to a favorite local swimming hole at McMillan Reservoir. Although this beats paying 10 bucks at Darlington, the fine if the ranger catches you might be a bit more costly.

The ride back goes through quiet towns including Allendale and Waldwick. Quite a bit of open space remains, and there are some horse farms mixed in among the townhouses and single-family developments. Many builders chose to leave the original trees standing, so a woodsy effect remains.

Directions to Starting Point: The **Ho-Ho-Kus Railroad Station** is several miles north of Paramus. Exit Rt. 17 onto Hollywood Ave. Turn left (west), crossing Rt. 17. Proceed to the first traffic light (Sheridan Ave.) and turn left. Look for Warren Ave., a small road immediately before the first group of shops in downtown Ho-Ho-Kus. Turn right and proceed two blocks to the train station. The parking lot at the station is reserved for commuters on weekdays, so park on the street if you are riding this route Monday through Friday.

PT.-PT.	CUME	DIRECTION	STREET/LANDMARK
0.0	0.0	S	**Warren Ave.** Bike over the green bridge
0.1	0.1	S	Cross Franklin Tpk. at stop sign
0.1	0.2	L	**Sheridan Ave.** (stop sign). Road will change name to **West Saddle River Rd.** as you enter Saddle River
2.4	2.6	R	**East Allendale Rd./County Rt. 90**
0.1	2.7	L	**East Saddle River Rd.**

PT.-PT.	CUME	DIRECTION	STREET/LANDMARK
1.9	4.6		**Elmer's Country Store** on left
0.9	5.5	L	**Old Stone Church Rd.**
0.7	6.2	R	**West Saddle River Rd.** (T)
0.2	6.4	L	**Sparrowbush Rd.**
0.6	7.0	BR	At fork, to continue on **Sparrowbush Rd.** (Carlough Rd. goes left)
0.2	7.2	S	Onto **East Crescent Ave.**
0.3	7.5	S	**Masonicus Rd.** (East Crescent Ave. goes left; head toward firehouse)
0.5	8.0	R	**Airmont Ave.** (T)
0.5	8.5	L	**Airmount Rd.**
1.0	9.5	S	At traffic light at bottom of hill, crossing Franklin Tpk. *CAUTION: One-lane underpass after this intersection. Often not enough room for an oncoming car and your bike!*
0.3	9.8	R	**Island Rd.** (T)
0.4	10.2	L	**West Ramapo Ave.**
0.1	10.3	L	Toward Rt. 17 South, crossing over Rt. 17
0.2	10.5	L	**Ridge Rd.** (T)
2.2	12.7	R	**Darlington Ave.** (T)
0.4	13.1		**Darlington County Park** on left
1.1	14.2	L	**Ramapo Valley Rd./Rt. 202** (T; no street sign). *CAUTION: Busy road*
0.1	14.3	R	**Ramapo Valley County Reservation.** After your visit to the park, return to **Rt. 202** and turn **left**, cycling back the way you came up
0.2	14.5	R	**Darlington Ave.**
0.2	14.7	R	**County Rt. 3/Campgaw Rd.**

PT.-PT.	CUME	DIRECTION	STREET/LANDMARK
2.0	16.7	L	**Youngs Rd.** Turn is where Campgaw Rd. widens to two lanes in your direction
0.5	17.2	R	**Chapel Rd.**
0.7	17.9	L	**Pulis Ave.** (stop sign)
0.9	18.8	S	Cross Wyckoff Ave. at traffic light. Road you will be on is **Forest Rd.**
0.8	19.6		**Deli** on left
0.2	19.8	R	**MacIntyre Lane.** Turn is just past narrow bridge
0.6	20.4	L	**Brookside Ave.** (T)
0.3	20.7	S	Cross West Crescent Ave. at traffic light. You are now on **County Rt. 101/Brookside Ave.**
0.3	21.0	L	**Park Ave.** (T)
0.1	21.1	R	Immediate right onto **Orchard St.**
0.3	21.4	R	**Franklin Tpk./Rt. 507** (T)
0.1	21.5	R	**Chestnut St.**
0.3	21.8		Road becomes **Hopper Ave.** as you enter Waldwick. *CAUTION: Railroad tracks cross road at dangerous angle*
0.7	22.5	S	Cross West Prospect St. at stop sign
0.1	22.6	L	**Wyckoff Ave.** (T; no street sign)
0.1	22.7	R	Immediate right at traffic light onto **Monroe St.**
0.4	23.1	L	**Hillcrest Rd.**
0.9	24.0	L	**Glenwood Rd.**
0.1	24.1	R	**Upper Blvd.** (T)
0.0	24.1	L	Immediate **left** onto unnamed road heading down toward railroad tracks. *CAUTION: Steep and curvy road. Control your speed!*
0.2	24.3	R	**Ho-Ho-Kus Railroad Station.** End of route

LIVINGSTON-WATCHUNG RESERVATION—27.8 MILES

White Meadow Press alumna Melissa Van Kueren suggested this route as a way to link the many arboretums and parks in the Livingston-Millburn-Summit area. It is a good beginner ride as well as an excellent after-work ride for fast cyclists who don't mind a few busy roads. Traffic has gotten quite a bit busier in this area in the past several years with the opening of the I-78 and Rt. 24 freeways, but there are enough quiet roads and points of interest to make this route worthwhile.

Terrain: Lightly rolling, for the most part, with a few steeper climbs and drops.

Traffic: Moderate on suburban streets. Somewhat busier during rush hour. This route is best pedaled early on weekend mornings if you are doing it for the scenery.

Road Conditions: Good to excellent, with a few bumpy shoulders.

Points of Interest: Reeves-Reed Arboretum; **Trailside Nature and Science Center**; **Watchung Reservation**; **Hartshorn Arboretum**; beautiful homes with manicured lawns in Short Hills and vicinity.

Sometimes it's nice to take a bike ride without having to drive far from home. For the many cyclists who live and work in western Essex County and eastern Morris County, this route offers pleasant suburban and wooded scenery and light-to-moderate traffic without having to haul the bike out to western New Jersey.

This is a good beginner ride, with only a few taxing climbs. There are a number of beautiful sights along the way. The Short Hills area has many pretty homes (mansions may be the proper word) with knockout landscaping that is especially nice in the spring as the big trees come into leaf.

Cycle south out of Livingston into Millburn. The wooded area on both sides of East Hobart Gap Road is a buffer zone for

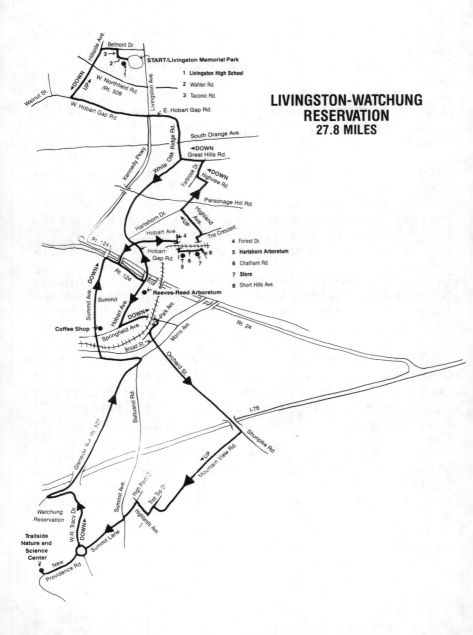

**LIVINGSTON-WATCHUNG
RESERVATION
27.8 MILES**

START/Livingston Memorial Park

1 Livingston High School
2 Wahler Rd.
3 Taconic Rd.

4 Forest Dr.
5 Hartshorn Arboretum
6 Chatham Rd.
7 Store
8 Short Hills Ave.

water company reservoirs. You might be lucky and see a deer cross the road early in the morning or at twilight.

Upon entering Summit, visit the first of two arboretums on this route. The Reeves-Reed Arboretum has formal and semi-formal gardens, a fabulous daffodil display in the spring, open fields and hillsides, and a hardwood forest with wildflowers.

Next, ride toward Watchung Reservation. This is not an Indian reservation but a large Union County park. The Trailside Science and Nature Museum (open after 1:00 p.m.) contains very interesting exhibits, and is a good spot to fill water bottles. The ride down W.R. Tracy Drive through the reservation is a smooth and fast descent—ample reward for the hill climbed on Mountain View Rd.

Return to Summit and then head into the center of Short Hills, where you can get a snack at the small food store by the train station. The Hartshorn Arboretum just before the food store has some beautiful rhododendron stands and small decorative fountains—worth getting off the bike for!

Back in the saddle (or out of it), climb Highland Ave. and pass the large estate-like homes that give this community its reputation as a wealthy, quiet place. Soon you'll be back in Livingston and the end of the route. A pretty ride in suburban New Jersey!

Directions to Starting Point: Livingston Memorial Park is on Livingston Ave. (Rt. 527), 2 miles south of I-280 Exit 5A and one mile south of Rt. 10. The park, which is in front of Livingston High School, is a right turn off Southbound Livingston Ave.

PT.-PT.	CUME	DIRECTION	STREET/LANDMARK
0.0	0.0		With the high school on your left and the Livingston Recreation and Parks office on your right, turn onto unmarked **Wahler Rd.** This will change its name to **Taconic Rd.**

0.3	0.3	**L**	**Belmont Dr.** (stop sign)
0.4	0.7	**L**	**Hillside Ave.** (T)
0.4	1.1	**S**	Cross W. Northfield Rd./Rt. 508 at traffic light
0.9	2.0	**L**	**West Hobart Gap Rd.** (T)
1.2	3.2	**S**	Cross Kennedy Pkwy. at traffic light onto **East Hobart Gap Rd./ Rt. 527 Spur**
1.0	4.2	**S**	Cross South Orange Ave. at traffic light onto **White Oak Ridge Rd.**
0.5	4.7	**R**	To continue on **White Oak Ridge Rd.** Great Hills Rd. goes straight
0.8	5.5	**S**	Cross Parsonage Hill Rd. at traffic light
1.5	7.0	**R**	At blinking yellow light (*comes up suddenly when descending a hill*) onto **Hobart Ave.**
0.2	7.2	**S**	At first stop sign, crossing over Rt. 24 freeway
0.1	7.3	**L**	At second stop sign, toward Rt. 24 East
0.1	7.4	**R**	**Hobart Ave.**, toward Summit (traffic light)
0.3	7.7		Entrance to **Reeves-Reed Arboretum** on left
0.5	8.2	**L**	At second stop sign onto **Springfield Ave.** (Note: Should you need **food**, turn right here instead and ride 0.3 miles into downtown Summit for a coffee shop)
0.6	8.8	**SR**	**Park Ave.** Turn is first right past railroad underpass. *CAUTION— you will be going fast down a hill at this point. Gently use your breaks to slow your speed before the turn!*
0.1	8.9	**L**	**Orchard St.** (street sign on right)
0.1	9.0	**S**	Cross Broad St. at stop sign

PT.-PT.	CUME	DIRECTION	STREET/LANDMARK
0.1	9.1	**S**	Cross Morris Ave. at traffic light. Road becomes **Shunpike Rd.**
0.7	9.8	**R**	**Mountain View Rd.** Turn is just past I-78 overpass
1.0	10.8	**L**	**Tree Top Dr.** (T)
0.2	11.0	**R**	**Highlands Ave.**
0.2	11.2	**L**	**Highpoint Dr.**
0.3	11.5	**L**	**Summit Ave.** (T, traffic light)
0.0	11.5	**R**	Immediate right onto **Summit Lane.** Don't miss this turn—you will regret climbing back up the Watchung ridge
0.8	12.3		Go halfway around the traffic circle, heading toward Berkeley Heights, New Providence and the Trailside Nature and Science Center. You will still be on **Summit Lane**, which will change its name to **New Providence Rd.**
0.6	12.9	**R**	Into **Trailside Nature and Science Center.** After visiting museum, exit **left** onto **New Providence Rd.**, cycling the way you came in
0.6	13.5		Go three-quarters of the way around the traffic circle, and turn onto **W.R. Tracy Dr.**
1.5	15.0	**R**	**Glenside Ave./Rt. 527 North** (T)
1.7	16.7	**BL**	At stop sign, to continue on **Glenside Ave.** Baltusrol Rd. goes right
0.1	16.8	**SL**	**Morris Ave.** (T)
0.4	17.2	**R**	**Summit Ave.** (first traffic light). Ride through downtown Summit
1.5	18.7	**R**	Onto **Rt. 24 Freeway Service Rd.**, toward Rt. 24 East

PT.-PT.	CUME	DIRECTION	STREET/LANDMARK
0.6	19.3	L	**Hobart Gap Rd.** (traffic light). Cross Rt. 24 freeway
0.2	19.5	R	**Hobart Ave.** (blinker light)
0.7	20.2	R	**Forest Dr.** (go under railroad)
0.1	20.3	L	**Chatham Rd.** (stop sign after railroad underpass). Note: For entrance to **Hartshorn Arboretum**, go **straight** here for 0.1 mile. Arboretum entrance is on left
0.1	20.4		**Store** on right (Village Pantry)
0.2	20.6	SL	At yield sign onto **Short Hills Ave.** Go under railroad
0.1	20.7	R	**The Crescent** (T)
0.1	20.8	S	**Highland Ave.** The Crescent goes right
1.0	21.8	R	**Hartshorn Dr.** (T)
0.1	21.9	S	Cross Parsonage Hill Rd. at traffic light
0.4	22.3	L	**Highview Rd.**
0.2	22.5	R	**Farbrook Dr.** (T)
0.3	22.8	L	**Great Hills Rd.** (stop sign)
0.3	23.1	S	onto **White Oak Ridge Rd.**
0.5	23.6	S	Cross South Orange Ave. at traffic light onto **East Hobart Gap Rd.**
1.1	24.7	S	Cross Kennedy Pkwy. at traffic light onto **West Hobart Gap Rd.**
1.1	25.8	R	**Hillside Ave.**
0.9	26.7	S	Cross W. Northfield Rd. at traffic light
0.4	27.1	R	**Belmont Dr.**
0.4	27.5	R	**Taconic Rd.** Road will change name to **Wahler Rd.**
0.3	27.8		**Livingston Memorial Park.** End of route

MONTCLAIR-BRANCH BROOK PARK—27.5 MILES

This route explores urban and old suburban territory, allowing cyclists to visit places unique to North Jersey, including Thomas Edison's labs and home, the huge estate-like homes of Montclair, and Branch Brook Park with its amazing display of cherry blossoms in April.

Terrain: Gently rolling, for the most part. A few short steep climbs.
Traffic: Mostly light on the way out to Branch Brook Park. Moderate and occasionally heavy on the way back, but there is always an adequate shoulder. (Note that even on lightly travelled streets, cross-streets may have heavy traffic so *heed all stop signs and traffic lights!*)
Road Conditions: Quite smooth and well-paved.
Points of Interest: Montclair Art Museum; **Edison National Historic Site**; **Glenmont (Edison home)**; **Branch Brook Park** (especially of interest the third weekend in April, which is **cherry blossom** time); **Cathedral of the Sacred Heart**; large homes on old, wide, tree-shaded streets in Montclair and Glen Ridge; **Presby Memorial Iris Garden** (peak display in late May and early June).

The area covered by *RIDE GUIDE/North Jersey* offers not only excellent rides in the country (passing field and babbling brook and lowing cow), but also offers rewarding cycling in older towns and suburbs, passing beautifully designed gardens, parks and historic landmarks.

This route features wide, quiet streets under huge old shade trees—a good setting for the enormous old homes of the first wealthy suburban settlers of the late 19th and early 20th Centuries. Glen Ridge streets are still lit by gaslamps—you almost expect a horse and buggy to go clip-clopping by.

Montclair lies under the Watchung Mountains, so expect an occasional hill, up or down, as you wind your way over to

Belleville and Newark. Before the trees are in leaf, you might
catch a glimpse of the New York skyline in the distance. The
first point of interest is Montclair Art Museum, which also has
a small arboretum on its grounds.

Next head into West Orange. Stop at the Edison National
Historic Site. The Visitor's Center is open 9 a.m. to 5 p.m., and
90-minute tours of the labs are given by rangers daily. This is a
very special tour and worth the time. You will see a replica of
the first motion picture studio, the inventor's restored office/
library and some of his early inventions. If you wish to tour or
just ride by Glenmont (Edison's home), obtain a pass at the
Visitor's Center. Home tours are very popular and are available
Wednesday through Sunday. Call (201) 736-0550 for more information.

Pass in hand, head to the gate of Llewellyn Park, one of the
first planned residential communities in the U.S. You must have
a pass to enter the park, and you can only ride to Glenmont. Do
not ride on the other streets, as these are private. Enjoy the
huge old stands of rhododendron and hemlock on the way up to
Glenmont. This is a beautiful, quiet enclave in the midst of busy
West Orange.

After leaving West Orange, head downhill through Glen
Ridge. Cycle through the pretty Bloomfield College campus, then
on to Branch Brook Park. During cherry blossom time (mid-
April), weekend park traffic is congested, otherwise the roads
are quiet. You will pass ponds and woods and old Italian men
playing bocce as you wend your way through an area that, incredibly enough, is within the city limits of Newark. At the south
end of the park is the Cathedral of the Sacred Heart, one of the
10 largest cathedrals in the world.

Return to Montclair on a slightly uphill course. Pass two
extraordinary parks in Montclair—Memorial Park, with its
World War I Veterans monument reflected in the lake, a highly
photogenic site, and Mountainside Park, home of the Presby
Memorial Iris Garden, which is world renowned for its 50,000
iris plantings featuring 6,000 varieties.

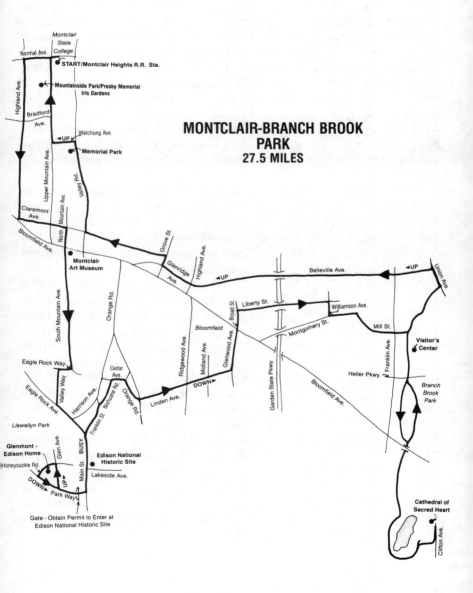

MONTCLAIR-BRANCH BROOK PARK
27.5 MILES

Montclair State College

Normal Ave.

● START/Montclair Heights R.R. Sta.

● ◀ Mountainside Park/Presby Memorial Iris Gardens

Highland Ave.

Bradford Ave.

Upper Mountain Ave.

◀UP

Watchung Ave.

● ◀ Memorial Park

Valley Rd.

North Mountain Ave.

Claremont Ave.

Bloomfield Ave.

● Montclair Art Museum

Grove St.

Glenridge Ave.

Highland Ave.

◀UP

Belleville Ave. ◀

◀UP

Union Ave.

South Mountain Ave.

Orange Rd.

Liberty St.

Broad St.

Williamson Ave.

Mill St.

Montgomery St.

● Visitor's Center

Bloomfield

Eagle Rock Way

Ridgewood Ave.

Midland Ave.

Glenwood Ave.

Garden State Pkwy.

Franklin Ave.

Heller Pkwy. ◀

Branch Brook Park

Cedar Ave.

Valley Way

Harrison Ave.

Franklin St. Nishuane Rd.

Orange Rd.

Linden Ave.

DOWN ▶

Bloomfield Ave.

Eagle Rock Ave.

Llewellyn Park

Glenmont - Edison Home

Glen Ave.

BUSY

Honeysuckle Rd.

Main St.

DOWN ▶ ▲UP

Park Way ▲

● Edison National Historic Site

Lakeside Ave.

Gate - Obtain Permit to Enter at Edison National Historic Site

Cathedral of Sacred Heart ●

Clifton Ave.

Directions to Starting Point: Montclair Heights Railroad Station is on Normal Ave., west of Valley Rd. Take Rt. 3 or 46 to the "Montclair" exit (just west of the intersection of these two highways), then head south one mile on Valley Rd. to the first traffic light and turn right. The train station will be on the left in two blocks. During the week, the parking lot by the station is reserved for permit-holding commuters, so park on the adjacent campus of Montclair State College.

PT.-PT.	CUME	DIRECTION	STREET/LANDMARK
0.0	0.0	L	Exit railroad station parking lot and turn **left** onto **Normal Ave.**, crossing tracks
0.2	0.2	L	**Highland Ave.** (first left past first traffic light)
1.0	1.2	S	Cross Bradford Ave. at stop sign
1.6	2.8	L	**Claremont Ave.** (T)
0.3	3.1	R	**North Mountain Ave.** (second traffic light)
0.2	3.3	S	Cross Bloomfield Ave. at traffic light onto **South Mountain Ave. Montclair Art Museum** on left after intersection
1.2	4.5	R	**Eagle Rock Way.** Turn is just before a curve in the road
0.1	4.6	L	**Valley Way**
0.6	5.2	L	**Eagle Rock Ave.** (T). Road changes name to **Main St.**
0.5	5.7		**Deli** on right
0.3	6.0	L	**Lakeside Ave.** Entrance to **Edison National Historic Site** will be on left. Obtain pass here to ride into Llewellyn Park and up to Glenmont. After visiting historic site, return to **Main St.** and turn **left**

PT.-PT.	CUME	DIRECTION	STREET/LANDMARK
0.2	6.2	**R**	At traffic light, into the gates of **Llewellyn Park**. Show pass to guard, then bear right up **Park Way**
0.3	6.5	**R**	**Glen Ave.**
0.1	6.6	**L**	Entrance to **Glenmont**, home of Thomas Edison. Turn is after speed bump. Honeysuckle Rd. goes right. House will be on your left (tours by reservation, made back at Visitors Center)
0.2	6.8	**L**	**Park Way** (T)
0.5	7.3	**L**	**Main St.** (traffic light)
0.6	7.9	**BR**	**Franklin St.** (second traffic light, no street sign). Pass old school on the right after turn
0.5	8.4	**BR**	**Nishuane Rd.** (fork)
0.3	8.7	**R**	**Cedar Ave.** (T)
0.3	9.0	**R**	Curve right onto **Orange Rd.**
0.2	9.2	**L**	**Linden Ave.** Caution: busy road. Walk bikes for left turn
0.4	9.6	**S**	Cross Ridgewood Ave. at stop sign
0.2	9.8	**S**	Cross Midland Ave. at stop sign
0.4	10.2	**L**	**Glenwood Ave.** (T)
0.3	10.5	**S**	Cross Bloomfield Ave. at the traffic light in the center of Bloomfield onto unmarked **Broad St.** (Woolworth's will be on your right)
0.1	10.6	**R**	**Liberty St.** (just past monument)
0.3	10.9		Cross over Garden State Pkwy.
0.2	11.1	**R**	**Williamson Ave.** (stop sign)
0.2	11.3	**L**	**Montgomery St.** (T)
0.4	11.7	**R**	**Mill St.** (stop sign)

PT.-PT.	CUME	DIRECTION	STREET/LANDMARK
0.5	12.2	S	At traffic light, crossing Franklin Ave. to enter **Branch Brook Park**
0.1	12.3	R	At T in park
0.3	12.6		**Restrooms** available at **visitor's center** on left. Bocce courts behind building
1.6	14.2	BR	At T (yield sign) to continue on park road. Go under underpass
1.3	15.5	R	At point where straight ahead is marked "No Motor Vehicles"
0.1	15.6	L	**Clifton Ave.** (T; no street sign)
0.1	15.7		**Cathedral of Sacred Heart** (visitor's entrance on left side of building). Then **U-turn** and return into park the way you came
4.0	19.7	L	**Union Ave.** (no street sign). This is the third traffic light. You are exiting the park at this point. Assembly Point Tavern on the corner
0.2	19.9	L	**Belleville Ave.** (traffic light; no street sign). Ice cream stand on left
1.7	21.6		Cross over Garden State Pkwy.
1.1	22.7	S	Cross Highland Ave. onto **Glenridge Ave.**
0.5	23.2	R	**Grove St.**
0.2	23.4	L	**Claremont Ave.**
0.8	24.2	R	**Valley Rd.**
0.9	25.1		**Memorial Park** on left
0.2	25.3	L	**Watchung Ave.** (traffic light past park)
0.4	25.7	R	**Upper Mountain Ave.** (T)
1.3	27.0		**Mountainside Park** and **Presby Memorial Iris Gardens** on left
0.4	27.4	R	**Normal Ave.** (traffic light)
0.1	27.5	R	Into **Montclair Heights Railroad Station.** End of route

RINGWOOD-WEST MILFORD—38.2 or 46.2 MILES

This pretty route features a state park and huge tracts of watershed land that are the heart of the proposed New Jersey Highlands reserve.

Terrain: Gently rolling while travelling north and south. Hilly while cycling east and west.
Traffic: Moderate to annoying on Rt. 511, extremely light on Clinton Rd., light to moderate elsewhere.
Road Conditions: Well-paved in most places, except for Rt. 511 west of Wanaque Reservoir, which has broken pavement.
Points of Interest: Quiet and traffic-free cycling on Clinton Rd; horse farms along West Brook Rd.; **Monksville Dam**; **Ringwood State Park (state botanical gardens; Shepherd Lake Beach; Ringwood Manor**).

Northern Passaic County has changed from a major iron-producing center (18th and 19th Centuries) to a resort area to a region of year-round lake homes and watershed property.

The presence of large tracts of undeveloped land designed to keep the water pure for the large cities of northern New Jersey is what makes this route enjoyable. Clinton Rd. is a nine-mile stretch of blacktop through Newark Watershed property that is as pretty and deserted as the Delaware Water Gap. Wanaque Reservoir is a large body of water surrounded by beautiful hills.

Start by cycling alongside Wanaque Reservoir (pronounced "Wanna-cue"). The road has an adequate shoulder here. In the early morning of a fall day, you might enjoy a breathtaking "reflection view" of autumn foliage on the still water. You will pass the site of Long Pond Ironworks, which the state is hoping to restore.

As you head into West Milford, traffic picks up and the shoulder deteriorates. The road into Upper Greenwood Lake is a major 1-mile climb.

Once up to the lake, turn south (and parallel to the ridges) on Clinton Rd. Pass numerous lakes and streams on this quiet stretch, and watch for deer and other wildlife.

Return to the area of Wanaque Reservoir on some hillier east-west roads. While the climb on Gould Rd. is taxing, the descent on West Brook Rd. is exhilarating and seems to go on forever. Be on the lookout for the many horse farms.

Stonetown Rd. includes another incredible downhill (after a short, steep climb), taking you down to and over the Monksville Dam. Stop at the observation platform at the far end of the dam for a good view of the hills surrounding Monksville and Wanaque Reservoirs.

After you return to the starting point, you may wish to tour the three units of Ringwood State Park. Using your bike will save you parking fees and add an enjoyable eight miles to the route.

Skylands Manor contains the New Jersey Botanical Garden. This is a unique huge formal garden containing many species of trees. The manor house itself is generally not open to the public. You will be cycling up a major hill to reach Skylands, but it will be your final climb of the trip. The bells you may hear in the distance are from the Mount St. Francis Retreat.

Shepherd Lake is a good place to cool off after that climb. This is an organized beach with showers and a changing room. You will briefly enter New York State on your way out of the lake area, and enjoy a nice descent back into New Jersey.

Ringwood Manor is a large 19th Century mansion owned by several prominent industrialists and iron kings of the time, including Robert Erskine, Peter Cooper, and Abram S. Hewitt. The manor house contains a museum and tours are available. The landscaped grounds are quite beautiful.

Directions to Starting Point: Eleanor C. Hewitt School is on Sloatsburg Rd. in Ringwood. From Bergen County and the Garden State Pkwy. take Rt. 4 West to Rt. 208 West to Skyline Dr. Or take I-287 to the Skyline Drive exit, which is just south of the junction with Rt. 208. At the end of Skyline Dr. take Rt.

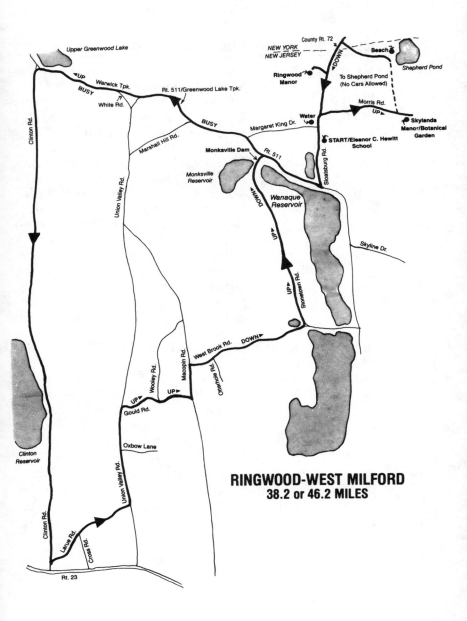

RINGWOOD-WEST MILFORD
38.2 or 46.2 MILES

511 North to the second right turn, which is Sloatsburg Rd. The school will be on your right in a little over a mile.

PT.-PT.	CUME	DIRECTION	STREET/LANDMARK
0.0	0.0	L	Exit school and turn left onto **Sloatsburg Rd.**
1.2	1.2	R	**Rt. 511** (T)
5.3	6.5	BR	To continue on **Rt. 511 North/ Greenwood Lake Tpk.** (Marshall Hill Rd. goes left)
1.6	8.1	BR	**Warwick Tpk.** (Union Valley Rd. goes left). **Deli** at center of fork
0.4	8.5	BR	To continue on **Warwick Tpk.** (White Rd. comes in from the left). Begin steep climb on busy road toward Upper Greenwood Lake
1.1	9.6		Hill ends as you enter Upper Greenwood Lake
0.8	10.4	L	**Clinton Rd.**
9.2	19.6	L	**Larue Rd.** (no street sign). Turn is immediately before the traffic light for Rt. 23
1.4	21.0	L	**Union Valley Rd.** (T)
1.8	22.8	R	**Gould Rd.**
2.2	25.0	L	**Macopin Rd.** (T)
1.1	26.1	R	**West Brook Rd.** No street sign! There is a sign for a campground. Turn is first right turn after Echo Lake Baptist Church
0.8	26.9	L	Curve left at fork (with Mobil Station in center) to continue on **West Brook Rd.** Otterhole Rd. goes right

PT.-PT.	CUME	DIRECTION	STREET/LANDMARK
4.3	31.2	**BL**	**Stonetown Rd.** No street sign! Turn is just after a stretch of road with fences on both sides of the road, just after you enter the property of Wanaque Reservoir
3.9	35.1	**R**	**Rt. 511** (T). Before you get to this intersection, watch speed on bumpy downhill approaching (and then crossing) **Monksville Dam**.
1.9	37.0	**L**	**Sloatsburg Rd.** (toward Ringwood State Park)
1.2	38.2		**Eleanor C. Hewitt School** on right. You may end your route here, or continue into Ringwood State Park
0.6	38.8		**Water fountain** available on left beyond building at ballfield (turn onto Margaret King Drive)
0.3	39.1	**R**	**Morris Rd.** toward Skylands Manor and Botanical Gardens. Begin major climb after passing Mount St. Francis Retreat
1.5	40.6		**Skylands Manor/Botanical Garden** entrance. Cycle back toward exit
0.1	40.7	**BR**	At fork, toward **Shepherd Lake**. Do not go down hill (road with Speed Limit 35 sign). Walk bike around barrier
0.8	41.5	**L**	After barricade. **Shepherd Lake**. You may swim here in season, or else make a second left to exit area (toward the small house in the center of the road used to collect parking fees)

PT.-PT.	CUME	DIRECTION	STREET/LANDMARK
1.2	42.7	**L**	At T onto unmarked **Orange County Rt. 72**, which becomes **Sloatsburg Rd.** when you re-enter New Jersey
1.9	44.6	**R**	**Ringwood Manor** entrance
0.2	44.8		**Museum** entrance. Cycle back the way you came in
0.2	45.0	**R**	**Sloatsburg Rd.** (T)
1.2	46.2	**L**	**Eleanor C. Hewitt School**. End of route

RIDES STARTING IN MORRIS COUNTY

About ten years ago weekend cyclists from more crowded points to the east could stop driving and start pedaling once they reached Morris County, happy in the knowledge that they were "in the country." That's not quite the case anymore with the rapid development of this historic, hilly, and beautiful county. Fortunately some of the nicer areas remain inviting as ever to cyclists, particularly in the southern parts of Morris adjoining Somerset and Hunterdon Counties.

Chester-Lebanon pedals through Morris County's still-rural southwest corner and into Hunterdon County. Enjoy many long and happy descents on this ride. One of the biggest uphills is almost painless, since it occurs on dirt roads climbing next to pretty gorges. Among the features of this route are a classic country store, a park with a swimming beach and a pick-your-own-apple farm.

Great Swamp is one of the flattest routes in *RIDE GUIDE*. The roads around the Swamp have gotten a little busier in recent years, but this still is an interesting tour, taking the rider to the wildlife observation boardwalk, Archie's Resale Shop in Meyersville, the Raptor Trust and along some quiet estates bordering the Swamp. An additional loop allows a two-wheeled visit to Washington's Headquarters and a spin along a bike path to Convent Station.

Jockey Hollow-Gladstone via Basking Ridge makes it possible to visit this corner of New Jersey without constantly climbing and descending hills. There are a couple of big ones, of course, but for the most part the route is rolling. En route you will pass pretty streamside vistas, an Audubon Society preserve, some small, quaint towns, a renowned garden (Leonard Buck Gardens), the U.S. Golf Association Museum, and many horses. You can combine this route with **Great Swamp** for a longer ride.

Jockey Hollow-Gladstone via Mendham connects the same two points as the ride above but is shorter with a greater altitude change. As a matter of challenge, the dreaded "Jacob's

Ladder" is included in this course. Wild raspberries growing along the roads will sustain you up the hills in summer. This route is good for touring Morristown National Historic Park (Jockey Hollow) and the hills to the north and west, as well as visiting the horse country around Gladstone and pretty Ravine Lake.

Rockaway Valley remains an undeveloped oasis very close to the busy Rt. 80 and Rt. 23 corridors. The opening of I-287 has reduced rush-hour traffic on the main north-south roads in this area. The ride, which heads north from Denville to Fayson Lakes, is remarkably flat on the north-south roads. It also explores the hills and horse farms just west of the valley, giving the cyclist a good workout.

CHESTER-LEBANON—42.8 MILES

A version of this route was initially designed by Art Portmore, a Morris Area Freewheeler who is known for his knack of finding scenic and challenging places to ride. We took out a few of the major challenges, and the result was this route, perfect for advanced novice and intermediate cyclists.

Terrain: Rolling, with only a few memorable climbs. In fact, it seems like you're mostly going downhill!
Traffic: Extremely light, except brief stretches on Rt. 24 and Naughright Rd., which have moderate traffic.
Road Conditions: Ranges from patchy pavement to good. One section of dirt road (Hollow Brook Rd.).
Points of Interest: Beautiful and remote backroads of southwestern Morris County and Hunterdon County's Lebanon Township; **Schooley's Mountain** and **Wood Glen General Stores**; **Teetertown Ravine Nature Preserve**; **Schooley's Mountain Park** (swimming); **Riamede Farms** (pick your own apples); the shops and eateries of **Chester**.

Defying physics and the law of gravity, cyclists on this route are lulled into thinking they are only going downhill without paying the price of uphill climbs.

The reason for this, perhaps, is that one uphill that pays the price is ridden on a dirt road through pretty Teetertown Ravine that's best ridden slowly anyway. It's so scenic in the ravine that you don't even notice the climb. Also, a major part of the necessary climbing is done while returning to Chester, when you know the end of the route is near, and another climb has the Wood Glen General Store at the top as a reward. The ascent up Schooley's Mountain is gradual on a road paralleling the South Branch of the Raritan River. So the only noticeable hills are the descents, which are long and glorious.

Begin by cycling out of Chester. River Road takes you up Schooley's Mountain so gently that you don't know you're climbing. Flocktown Road is the first of many nice "wheeee" downhills.

The Schooley's Mountain General Store is one of two old-fashioned general stores this route passes. Note the pot-bellied stove in the middle of the floor. Cycle down Pleasant Grove Rd. and watch for the turn onto Mt. Lebanon Rd. or you will end up way down in the Musconetcong River Valley and have to climb back up.

After snaking around some narrow, scenic roads of Lebanon Township, where you see more open space than you thought existed in New Jersey, emerge at the Wood Glen General Store. This popular place, known for its homemade pies, is now open on Sunday.

Next you'll climb through the Teetertown Ravine Nature Preserve. The dirt road is rough and even the most experienced cyclists may have to walk some stretches because it is steep and traction is poor. Bring bug repellent in summer, and a camera at all times as the stream is very pretty as it tumbles down through the wooded glen.

Return to Morris County at the top of this ravine. Your next stop is Schooley's Mountain Park, which has a nice lake and public swimming beach, perfect on a warm summer day. The ride down the mountain is down somewhat busy Naughright Rd. Keep your speed under control on this steep road, and watch for "bike-killer" parallel storm drains that will eat you and your front wheel.

Right near the end of the route is a pick-your-own-apple orchard for autumn diversion. When you come back to the starting point, you may wish to bike or drive 1 mile west on Rt. 24 into downtown Chester. This is a pretty town with many interesting craft shops and several good restaurants.

Directions to Starting Point: The route begins at the **junction of Rts. 24 and 513** in Chester. This is about 12 miles west of Morristown (I-287 Exit 35) on Rt. 24 and 1 mile east of the junctions of Rts. 24 and 206 in downtown Chester. Parking

CHESTER-LEBANON
42.8 MILES

is available in an unpaved lot adjacent to Nelson's Cycle Shop off Rt. 24 just west of the intersection.

PT.-PT.	CUME	DIRECTION	STREET/LANDMARK
0.0	0.0		From the traffic light at the intersection of Rts. 24 and 513 in Chester, proceed down **Oakdale Rd.** Mobil station will be on your left
1.1	1.1	S	Cross Pleasant Hill Rd.
0.4	1.5	R	**Hillside Rd.** (T)
0.8	2.3	S	Cross Rt. 206 at traffic light onto unmarked **S. Four Bridges Rd.**
1.0	3.3	R	**Bartley Rd.** (T)
1.2	4.5	L	At yield sign and T (no street signs) to continue on **Bartley Rd.**
0.3	4.8	L	**River Rd.** (main road curves right). Pass Woof 'n' Purr Inn on your left after turn
3.2	8.0	L	**Springtown Rd.** (T)
0.7	8.7	R	**Flocktown Rd.**
1.7	10.4	S	Cross Naughright Rd. at stop sign
1.8	12.2	L	**Schooley's Mt. Rd./Rt. 24** (stop sign)
0.2	12.4		**Schooley's Mt. General Store** on left
0.1	12.5	R	**Pleasant Grove Rd.**
3.4	15.9	L	**Mt. Lebanon Rd.** Street sign is on the right. Watch for this turn! It is in the midst of a downhill, and if you miss it, you'll have a long way to climb back up. Mt. Lebanon Rd. is narrow with some poor pavement
1.5	17.4	L	**Sharrer Rd.**

PT.-PT.	CUME	DIRECTION	STREET/LANDMARK
1.6	19.0	**SR**	**Pleasant Grove Rd.** (yield sign; no street sign)
0.7	19.7	**R**	**Sliker Rd.** (T). *CAUTION: Intersection comes up quickly at end of curvy downhill*
0.7	20.4	**L**	Sharp curve left onto **Anthony Rd.**
2.6	23.0	**L**	**Newport Rd.**
0.2	23.2	**L**	At unmarked Y fork to continue on **Newport Rd.** Dewey Lane goes right
0.8	24.0	**L**	**Red Mill Rd.** (T). Climb
1.3	25.3	**L**	**W. Hill Rd.** (T). Becomes **Hill Rd. East**
0.1	25.4		**Wood Glen General Store** on left
2.1	27.5	**L**	**Sliker Rd.** (T). *As you approach this intersection on Hill Rd. East, be sure to control your speed. Downhill feeds into a one-lane bridge*
0.2	27.7	**R**	**Teetertown Rd.** No street sign! This road is the first right turn you encounter
0.6	28.3	**L**	Curve left to continue on **Teetertown Rd.** Maple Lane goes right
0.3	28.6	**L**	**Hollow Brook Rd.** (T). After you pass Ravine Rd., begin ascent on unpaved road through Teetertown Ravine
1.0	29.6	**L**	Curve left to continue on **Hollow Brook Rd.** Skytop Rd. goes right. Pavement returns. Go up short, incredibly steep climb
0.3	29.9	**R**	At unmarked T onto **Califon Rd.**

PT.-PT.	CUME	DIRECTION	STREET/LANDMARK
1.3	31.2	R	**Pleasant Grove Rd.** (stop sign)
1.5	32.7	R	**Wehrli Rd.**
1.2	33.9	L	**W. Springtown Rd.** (T)
0.5	34.4	S	Cross Schooley's Mt. Rd./Rt. 24 at stop sign onto **E. Springtown Rd.**
0.7	35.1	L	At stop sign at bottom of hill to continue on **E. Springtown Rd.** Camp Washington Rd. goes right
0.3	35.4		Entrance to **Schooley's Mt. Park** on right (swimming/bathrooms/water)
0.4	35.8	R	**Naughright Rd.** (T). *DANGER! Steep descent begins less than a mile from this intersection, with curves, traffic and "wheel-eater" storm drains. Control your speed!*
2.4	38.2	L	**Bartley Rd.** (T)
1.3	39.5	R	**S. Four Bridges Rd.**
1.0	40.5	S	Cross Rt. 206 at traffic light onto **Hillside Rd.**
0.9	41.4	L	**Oakdale Rd.**
0.3	41.7	S	Cross Pleasant Hill Rd.
0.3	42.0		**Riamede Farms** (pick your own apples in season) on left
0.8	42.8		**Junction of Rts. 24 and 513.** End of route

GREAT SWAMP — 27.3 or 34.2 MILES

*Portions of this ride constitute the traditional "D" or beginner's ride for the Morris Area Freewheelers. For years before winter riding became stylish, the bike club scheduled this ride in March. It is perfect for shaking the cobwebs out of the winterized body, and good anytime as a family ride or a lazy sightseeing tour, because there's a lot to see—especially if you're an animal lover. A longer, combined tour (59.6 or 66.5 miles) is possible. See **Jockey Hollow-Gladstone via Basking Ridge**, page 65.*

Terrain: Mostly flat. A few rollers near the beginning and end, and around the Passaic River Valley.
Traffic: Certain roads are busy at rush hour, but those roads are otherwise moderate. A good part of the route is on bike paths and a road that's closed to through traffic.
Road Conditions: Good to excellent. Under two miles of well-packed gravel on Pleasant Plains Rd.
Points of Interest: Loantaka Brook Reservation bike path and duck pond; **Great Swamp Wildlife Observation Center** (bird blind and boardwalk); **The Raptor Trust**; **Washington's Headquarters** (Ford Mansion and Museum, part of Morristown National Historic Park).

Congratulations! You have picked one of the flattest bike routes in northern New Jersey. If you dislike hills, this is the ride for you.

The reason for all this flatness southeast of Morristown is the Great Swamp. Around the time of the last ice age, this area was a lake. Now it is a large wilderness area in the midst of the suburbs, full of trees, ponds, and rivers and many species of animals, birds, mammals such as deer, muskrats and rabbits, and other interesting creatures including turtles of all types. Chances are very good you will see wildlife close up, especially if you ride early in the morning. And if you don't see any wild animals, you are almost guaranteed to see horses and sheep grazing on the Harding Township estates along the quiet back roads near the beginning and end of the route.

Start by travelling the 3.8-mile length of the Loantaka Brook Reservation bike path. If you are here very early in the morning you might catch sight of a blue heron or egret in the duck pond mixed in with all the geese and ducks. Ride slowly, and watch out for joggers and little children on tricycles.

Cycle around the periphery of the Swamp on quiet roads. The small, horsey estates here seem much farther than 30 miles from the Big Apple. Their owners are very glad that a proposed airport wasn't built here in the early 1960s.

Long Hill Rd. is a busy road during rush hour, but otherwise traffic is moderate. Be sure to stop at the Wildlife Observation Center—a boardwalk goes right into the Swamp to a bird blind.

The hamlet of Meyersville contains a general store that is a popular cyclist stopping point. If you're here on the weekends, you might wish to visit Archie's Resale Shop. Archie, who looks like Santa Claus, has the contents of everybody's attics in his yard, an interesting collection of animals out back, and is an excellent source of used children's ice skates.

After looping around the Passaic River Valley, the next point of interest is the Raptor Trust. This private organization helps injured hawks and owls mend and has a large collection of these birds.

Pleasant Plains Road is a gravel road going through the heart of the Great Swamp, and it is here that you're most likely to see wildlife, especially turtles crossing the road. It is closed to automobile through traffic, but bikes can squeeze through the gate on the bridge. Because this road is gravel and you'll have no choice but to ride slowly, it might be advisable to pack some insect repellent in the warm-weather months, as the horseflies love sweet, sweaty cyclists.

Return to Loantaka Brook Reservation via one semi-busy road (Lee's Hill) and several quiet back roads. If you are interested in seeing Washington's Headquarters and museum (open daily 9 a.m. to 5 p.m.), continue past the starting point on the

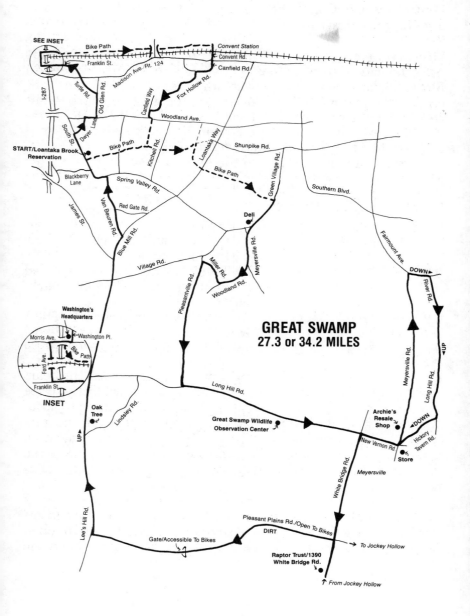

SEE INSET

Bike Path

Convent Station

Franklin St.

Convent Rd.

Madison Ave./Rt. 124

Canfield Rd.

Turtle Rd.

Old Glen Rd.

Fox Hollow Rd.

I-287

Canfield Way

Woodland Ave.

Dwyer Lane

South St.

Bike Path

Kitchell Rd.

Shunpike Rd.

Loantaka Way

START/Loantaka Brook Reservation

Green Village Rd.

Bike Path

Southern Blvd.

Blackberry Lane

Spring Valley Rd.

James St.

Red Gate Rd.

Deli

Van Buren Rd.

Blue Mill Rd.

Meyersville Rd.

Fairmount Ave.

DOWN

Village Rd.

Miller Rd.

Woodland Rd.

River Rd.

Washington's Headquarters

Morris Ave.

Washington Pl.

Ford Ave.

Bike Path

Franklin St.

INSET

GREAT SWAMP
27.3 or 34.2 MILES

Meyersville Rd.

UP

Long Hill Rd.

Oak Tree

Lindsley Rd.

Long Hill Rd.

Archie's Resale Shop

DOWN

UP

Great Swamp Wildlife Observation Center

New Vernon Rd.

Hickory Tavern Rd.

Store

White Bridge Rd.

Meyersville

Lee's Hill Rd.

Pleasant Plains Rd./Open To Bikes

DIRT

To Jockey Hollow

Gate/Accessible To Bikes

Raptor Trust/1390 White Bridge Rd.

From Jockey Hollow

route extension. This extra loop includes some beautiful residential areas in Convent Station and a two-mile bike path paralleling the railroad tracks.

Directions to Starting Point: South Street parking lot of Loantaka Brook Reservation is on South Street in Morristown. From I-287 southbound, use Exit 35. Turn right on Rt. 124 (Old Rt. 24/Madison Ave.), then make a sharp left at the next light onto South Street. Proceed 1 mile to the park, which is on your left just past Seaton Hackney stables. From I-287 northbound, Exit 35 puts you directly onto South Street. Turn right, and go 3/4 mile to the park, on your left.

PT.-PT.	CUME	DIRECTION	STREET/LANDMARK
0.0	0.0	S	Onto **Loantaka Brook Reservation Bike Path.** Path begins near parking lot entrance
0.7	0.7	S	At duck pond area. Proceed straight through circle and parking lot
0.2	0.9	L	At stop sign at unmarked **Kitchell Rd.**
0.0	0.9	R	Immediate right to continue on **bike path**
0.2	1.1		Path fords a stream. You may walk on concrete "stumps" while wheeling your bike through the water, or simply ride through
0.8	1.9	R	At unmarked four-way bike path intersection in the middle of the woods, take the path to the **right**
0.5	2.4	S	Cross unmarked Loantaka Way

PT.-PT.	CUME	DIRECTION	STREET/LANDMARK
1.4	3.8	**R**	At end of bike path onto unmarked **Green Village Rd.** You'll have to walk your bike through metal railings designed to keep all other types of vehicles off the bike path. The tiny Green Village post office is on your right after the turn
0.8	4.6	**L**	**Meyersville Rd.** Turn is just past **deli** (on right)
0.3	4.9	**R**	**Woodland Rd.**
0.6	5.5	**R**	**Miller Rd.**
0.4	5.9	**L**	**Pleasantville Rd.** (T)
1.8	7.7	**L**	**Long Hill Rd.** (T)
1.4	9.1		**Great Swamp Wildlife Observation Center** on right
1.9	11.0	**L**	**Meyersville Rd.** (stop sign). The road you were on has changed name to New Vernon Rd. **General Store** straight ahead of you at intersection. **Archie's Resale Shop** on left after you make turn
2.4	13.4	**R**	**Fairmount Ave.** (T)
0.3	13.7	**R**	**River Rd.** (stop sign at bottom of hill). Road changes name to **Long Hill Rd.** as you gradually ascend out of the Passaic River Valley
2.1	15.8	**R**	**Hickory Tavern Rd.** Control speed on downhill
0.6	16.4	**S**	At stop sign in Meyersville (**General Store** on your left). Cross Meyersville Rd. onto **New Vernon Rd.**
0.9	17.3	**L**	**White Bridge Rd.**

PT.-PT.	CUME	DIRECTION	STREET/LANDMARK
1.2	18.5	S	Cross Pleasant Plains Rd. *Cyclists combining this route with* **Jockey Hollow-Gladstone via Basking Ridge,** *turn* **left** *here. Return to* **Jockey Hollow** *route cue sheet, Mile 10.0, page 68*
0.2	18.7	R	Into **Raptor Trust** (1390 White Bridge Rd., about the third driveway past Pleasant Plains Rd. intersection). After visiting Raptor Trust, return the way you came (turning **left** onto **White Bridge Rd.**)
0.2	18.9	L	**Pleasant Plains Rd.** Ignore "Bridge Closed" signs—bikes can get through
0.4	19.3		Road becomes gravel
1.4	20.7		Squeeze bike (and yourself) through right side of gate on bridge. Pavement returns
1.0	21.7	R	**Lee's Hill Rd.** (T)
1.5	23.2		Enormous white oak tree on right, in field, just past Lindsley Rd. intersection. Good place to break up the climb with a rest
1.0	24.2	S	At traffic light, crossing Village Rd. Road changes name to **Blue Mill Rd.**
1.1	25.3	L	**Van Beuren Rd.**
1.5	26.8	L	**Spring Valley Rd.** (T)
0.3	27.1	R	Curve right. Road becomes **South St.**
0.2	27.3		**Loantaka Brook Reservation** on right. End of short route. Continue straight on **South St.** if you

PT.-PT.	CUME	DIRECTION	STREET/LANDMARK
			are doing the loop to Washington's Headquarters
0.4	27.7	R	**Dwyer Lane**
0.2	27.9	R	**Woodland Ave.** (stop sign)
0.1	28.0	L	**Old Glen Rd.**
0.4	28.4	L	**Turtle Rd.** (toward Woodland School)
0.5	28.9	S	At traffic light. Cross old Rt. 24/Madison Ave. Road becomes **Franklin St.**
0.6	29.5	R	**Ford Ave.** (turn is just past I-287 overpass)
0.3	29.8	R	**Morris Ave.** (T; traffic light, no street sign). *CAUTION: Very busy road!* Cross I-287
0.1	29.9		After admiring statue of Washington on horseback (on right), WALK your bike across Morris Ave., then WALK your bike along sidewalk. Turn **left** on **Washington Place**, and carefully walk bike against one-way traffic
0.2	30.1	L	Into "reserved parking" area. This will take you to door of museum at **Washington's Headquarters**. After touring the museum and Ford Mansion, return out to **Washington Place** and turn **right**
0.1	30.2	R	**Morris Ave.** WALK bike on sidewalk, as this is a one-way busy road going the wrong way
0.1	30.3		At end of Ford Mansion property, WALK bike across Morris Ave. and enter **bike route**

PT.-PT.	CUME	DIRECTION	STREET/LANDMARK
0.1	30.4		Be careful of chain stretched across bike route to prevent vehicular access. Continue **straight** on **bike route**, which will eventually parallel railroad tracks
1.7	32.1	**R**	At T at end of bike path onto unmarked **Convent Rd.** Entrance to College of St. Elizabeth is on your left. Cross tracks by Convent Station railroad station
0.2	32.3	**S**	Cross Rt. 124/Madison Ave. at traffic light onto **Canfield Rd.**
0.2	32.5	**L**	**Fox Hollow Rd.** Road is narrow and easy to miss. If you pass a large house with a white picket fence in front (on left), you've gone too far
0.4	32.9	**L**	**Canfield Way** (T at bottom of hill)
0.1	33.0	**L**	**Woodland Ave.** (T)
0.0	33.0	**R**	Immediate right onto **bike path**
0.5	33.5	**R**	Turn **right** just past the bathrooms (by the duck pond) to continue on **bike path.** Do not enter parking lot
0.7	34.2		**South St. parking lot** of Loantaka Brook Reservation. End of route

JOCKEY HOLLOW-GLADSTONE via BASKING RIDGE— 32.3 MILES

This is one of two routes linking Jockey Hollow and Gladsone. While longer, this course is actually easier because it has fewer hills. Cyclists seeking a longer day of riding can combine this route with **Great Swamp** *trip (page 57) for a 59.6 or 66.5 mile ride.*

Terrain: Rolling in between Jockey Hollow and Basking Ridge and Gladstone and Jockey Hollow, with a couple of steep climbs; otherwise, flat to gently rolling.
Traffic: Light to moderate.
Road Conditions: Fair to good, with occasional bumpy stretches. One short stretch (0.3 miles) of dirt road on Lord Stirling Rd.
Points of Interest: Jockey Hollow (Morristown National Historic Park); **Scherman Sanctuary/New Jersey Audubon Society** tract (hiking); **Somerset County Environmental Education Center** (exhibits, boardwalk); **Raptor Trust**; interesting towns of **Millington** and **Gladstone**; **U.S. Golf Association museum; Leonard Buck Gardens**; beautiful horse country riding.

Riding in the Jockey Hollow area does not mean you must have superior climbing ability. There are roads that do not climb over every hill and dale, yet still pass by the pretty woods and horse farms that abound in these parts. This route takes you to Gladstone via the flatter reaches of the Great Swamp, Basking Ridge, and the area around the V.A. Hospital in Lyons.

Exit Jockey Hollow immediately and head over one of the two long climbs of the route, up to the New Jersey Brigade area. Wild raspberries grow everywhere and are ripe for the picking in the summer.

It's all downhill to Basking Ridge along pretty Hardscrabble Road. Stop and look around at the Audubon Society's wildlife refuge, with its fields and woods abounding in deer.

Next head into the Great Swamp on Lord Stirling Road. The Somerset County Environmental Education Center has some interesting exhibits on the flora and fauna found in the Swamp, and you can walk into the wetlands on a boardwalk.

The Raptor Trust is on the left a little further down the same road. This is a private organization that is interested in hawks, eagles, owls, and other birds of prey.

Ride up a short hill to leave the flat Great Swamp. The small hamlet of Millington is next, with some pretty houses in wooded settings and a cafe in the railroad station.

Next cycle by the V.A. Hospital in Lyons, and on to Liberty Corner, a rural crossroads that maintains its character despite the growth in the surrounding area. On the road to Far Hills, there are two points of interest: the headquarters and museum of the U.S. Golf Association and Leonard Buck Gardens, where plants and flowers grow on rock outcroppings.

Far Hills to Gladstone is a gently rolling course through horse country. There is a pleasant park in Gladstone for lunch, but beware of the nasty swans who don't like cyclists intruding on their territory. The ride back to Jockey Hollow is a bit hillier, including one short steep climb on Cherry Lane by a pretty farm with the Mendham church steeple visible in the distance.

Directions to Starting Point: Morristown National Historic Park (Jockey Hollow) Visitor's Center is off Tempe Wick Rd., south of Morristown. From I-287, use the Harter Rd. exit. Turn left at the end of the ramp, proceed to the stop sign, then turn left on Rt. 202. In several miles you'll reach the traffic light, which is Tempe Wick Rd. Turn right, and the entrance to the park is a right turn in a little over a mile.

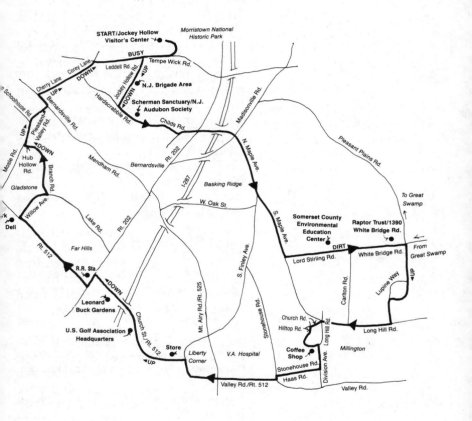

JOCKEY HOLLOW-
GLADSTONE VIA BASKING
RIDGE
32.3 MILES

PT.-PT.	CUME	DIRECTION	STREET/LANDMARK
0.0	0.0		Exit Visitor's Center toward Tempe Wick Rd., down the route you drove up on
0.3	0.3	R	**Tempe Wick Rd.** (T, no street sign), toward Mendham
0.7	1.0	L	**Leddell Rd.** Road will change name to **Jockey Hollow Rd.**
1.2	2.2		**New Jersey Brigade Area** on left at top of hill (no facilities)
0.5	2.7	L	**Hardscrabble Rd.** (T)
0.8	3.5		**Scherman Sanctuary/New Jersey Audubon Society** on left
1.1	4.6	L	**Childs Rd.** (T)
0.2	4.8	S	Cross Rt. 202 at traffic light onto **North Maple Ave.**
1.8	6.6	BL	At fork in Basking Ridge, onto **South Maple Ave.**, toward Millington
1.1	7.7	L	**Lord Stirling Rd.**, toward Great Swamp Refuge
1.0	8.7		**Somerset County Environmental Education Center** on left (exhibits, boardwalk, restrooms, water). Road becomes dirt immediately thereafter
0.3	9.0		Pavement returns. Road has changed name to **White Bridge Rd.**
0.7	9.7		**Raptor Trust** (1390 White Bridge Rd.) on left
0.3	10.0	R	**Pleasant Plains Rd.** *For cyclists combining this ride with the **Great Swamp** route, turn left at this corner instead and join the **Great***

PT.-PT.	CUME	DIRECTION	STREET/LANDMARK
			Swamp route at Mile 18.9 of its cue sheet, page 62
1.3	11.3	**L**	At T and stop sign, to continue on **Pleasant Plains Rd.** Lupine Way goes right
0.2	11.5	**R**	**Long Hill Rd.** (stop sign), toward Millington
1.0	12.5	**BL**	**Church Rd.** (at blinking light). Long Hill Rd. goes left, Basking Ridge Rd. goes straight
0.3	12.8	**L**	**Hilltop Rd.** at stop sign. *CAUTION: Watch speed on steep, winding downhill*
0.3	13.1	**R**	**Division Ave.**, crossing railroad tracks. **Cafe** in train station, on right
0.1	13.2	**R**	**Stonehouse Rd.** Street sign hidden behind tree. Beige stucco house (professional offices) on corner. Road will change name to **Haas Rd.** after crossing Passaic River
1.0	14.2	**L**	**Stonehouse Rd.** (T)
0.1	14.3	**R**	**Valley Rd.**
2.0	16.3	**S**	At traffic light, to continue on **Valley Rd./Rt. 512 West.** Cross Mt. Airy Rd.
0.4	16.7	**L**	**Church St./Rt. 512 West** at center of Liberty Corner. **Store** on right 0.1 miles after turn
1.7	18.4		**U.S. Golf Association headquarters and museum** on left
1.2	19.6		**Leonard Buck Gardens** on left

PT.-PT.	CUME	DIRECTION	STREET/LANDMARK
0.9	20.5	L	**Rt. 202 South** (T). **Restaurant** and bathrooms in Far Hills train station, on right after turn
0.3	20.8	R	**Rt. 512 West**, toward Peapack
2.6	23.4	R	**Willow Ave. Deli** on left at turn. A **park** is beyond the deli on Rt. 512, on the left
1.1	24.5	L	**Branch Rd.** Road will change name to **Hub Hollow Rd.**
1.5	26.0	R	**Mosle Rd.** (T)
0.6	26.6	BR	**Pleasant Valley Rd.** at yield sign. Union Schoolhouse Rd. goes left
1.6	28.2	L	**Bernardsville Rd.** (T)
0.5	28.7	BR	**Cherry Lane** (no street sign). Main road goes left, and Cherry Lane is narrow road between two fences that goes up short, steep hill shortly after turn. Road will change name to **Corey Lane**
2.2	30.9	R	**Tempe Wick Rd.** (stop sign)
1.1	32.0	L	Into **Morristown National Historic Park**
0.3	32.3		**Visitor's Center Parking Lot.** End of route

JOCKEY HOLLOW-GLADSTONE via MENDHAM—29.3 MILES

One of two routes linking Jockey Hollow and Gladstone, the Mendham routing was inspired by Morris Area Freewheeler Art Portmore's Halloween ride. If you ride this route on Halloween, be sure to cycle in costume!

Terrain: Hilly to downright mountainous in places. The mileage is kept short because of the elevation changes. "Jacob's Ladder" is a particularly feared ascent.
Traffic: Extremely light, except on Tempe Wick Rd. at the end of the route, which is moderate.
Road Conditions: Often choppy (wealthy towns in this area don't care to encourage fast traffic by maintaining smooth roads).
Points of Interest: Morristown National Historic Park (Wick House and soldier huts); beautiful horse country back roads; **Ralston General Store** (exhibit of 18th Century store open Sunday afternoons spring and fall); **Gladstone**, the shopping town for country squires; wild **raspberries** in July and August.

Jockey Hollow is a woodsy, deer-filled area beckoning the cycle tourist who doesn't mind climbing some bodacious hills along the way. Of course you'll also enjoy some fast, delicious descents—and even a few roads that qualify as "rolling." If you are riding in July or August, the roadsides are covered with sweet, bright red raspberries. These wild berries somehow take the sting out of the climbs.

Start at the Visitor's Center Parking Lot. When you return after the ride, look into the Visitor's Center and adjacent Wick House for good presentations of what life was like for the Revolutionary era soldier and farmer during the tough winters that Washington camped his troops here.

In a mile you'll encounter a group of reconstructed soldier huts. Rangers dressed in rags like those worn by soldiers give talks on life for the ordinary colonial soldier. Life for the cyclist is easier. You can fill your water bottles at the pump near the parking lot.

After a few more ups and downs, enjoy a view toward Mendham. Head downhill into the Washington Valley. A reservoir is proposed for this area, but right now it is home to horse farms and large estates—even a couple of cattle farms. You will pass the pretty hamlet of Brookside while cycling through the valley.

Skirt downtown Mendham on Mountainside Rd. then head toward Gladstone on Roxiticus Rd. Pass an amazing menagerie of animals on one farm—donkey, sheep, horses, and an enormous sow (with cute piglets in the spring) are all out there waiting for you to say hello.

Gladstone has a couple of food stores and a pleasant park for lunching (beware of the swans in the pond, they have been known to bite bike tires and bikers).

Cycle by beautiful Ravine Lake, then prepare for some quadriceps-testing climbs, including "Jacob's Ladder," so named because of the flat "steps" built into the rise, presumably to rest the horses that first suffered on this road. On the outskirts of Bernardsville, you'll zoom down Lloyd Rd., but then go up and down on Jockey Hollow Rd. It can be a tough fight against gravity here, but soon you're back at your car. Congratulations— you've conquered the hills.

Directions to Starting Point: Morristown National Historic Park (Jockey Hollow) Visitor's Center is off Tempe Wick Rd., south of Morristown. From I-287, use the Harter Rd. exit. Turn left at the end of the ramp, proceed to the stop sign, then turn left on Rt. 202. In several miles you'll reach the traffic light which is Tempe Wick Rd. Turn right, and the entrance to the park is a right turn in a little over a mile.

JOCKEY HOLLOW-
GLADSTONE VIA MENDHAM
29.3 MILES

PT.-PT.	CUME	DIRECTION	STREET/LANDMARK
0.0	0.0	S	**Tour Rd.**
1.2	1.2	L	At fork by **Soldier Huts** (which are straight ahead of you), toward Lewis Morris Park and Morristown. **Water pump** on left before fork
0.5	1.7	S	At entrance to Lewis Morris County Park (on left)
0.8	2.5	L	**Jockey Hollow Rd.** toward Morristown (T)
0.8	3.3	L	**Picatinny Rd.**
0.3	3.6		**View** on left toward Mendham. *CAUTION: Steep hill after this—control speed, stop sign and busy road at the bottom*
0.8	4.4	L	**Mendham Rd./Rt. 24** (T)
0.2	4.6	R	**Washington Valley Rd.**
2.9	7.5	L	**Tingley Rd.** (T)
0.3	7.8	R	**East Main St.** Turn is in the midst of a descent
0.6	8.4	S	At intersection in middle of Brookside to continue on **West Main St.** Pass yellow former school building on left after intersection
1.0	9.4	R	**Cold Hill Rd.** (T)
0.1	9.5	L	**Mountainside Rd.**
1.3	10.8	S	Cross Calais Rd. at stop sign. *CAUTION: After this intersection there is a brief, winding, intensely steep downhill. Watch your speed!*
0.9	11.7	L	**Ironia Rd.** (T)
0.6	12.3	R	**Roxiticus Rd.** at fork

PT.-PT.	CUME	DIRECTION	STREET/LANDMARK
0.4	12.7	S	Cross Rt. 24 at stop sign. **Ralston General Store** (exhibit) on left before crossing highway
1.1	13.8		**Menagerie** farm on right. Look for the biggest sow you've ever seen!
3.2	17.0	R	**Dewey Ave.** Road you were on has changed name to Mendham Rd. as you entered Gladstone
0.1	17.1	L	**Main St.** (T). **Deli** on right after turn
0.4	17.5	R	**Mendham Rd./Rt. 512 East** (T)
0.2	17.7		**Park** on right
0.1	17.8	L	**Willow Ave. Deli** on right just before turn
1.5	19.3	BR	At fork after crossing bridge (no street signs). Head toward Ravine Lake
1.9	21.2	L	Unmarked **Post Kennel Rd.** Turn is just past green gate (on right) and is first left past "No Outlet" left turn (Hidden Valley Rd.). Climb Jacob's Ladder
1.7	22.9	BL	**Roebling Rd.** (stop sign)
0.6	23.5	R	**Mountain Top Rd.** (T)
0.7	24.2	R	**Post Lane**
0.5	24.7	R	**Claremont Rd.** (T)
0.0	24.7	L	Immediate left onto **Ballantine Rd.**
0.6	25.3	BR	At fork during downhill onto unmarked **Pfizer Rd.**
0.2	25.5	R	**Mendham Rd.** (T)
0.2	25.7	L	**Lloyd Rd.**
0.7	26.4	R	**Hardscrabble Rd.** (T; no street sign)

PT.-PT.	CUME	DIRECTION	STREET/LANDMARK
0.1	26.5	L	**Jockey Hollow Rd.** (first left turn; no street sign)
0.5	27.0		**New Jersey Brigade Area** on right (no facilities). Watch your speed on the next downhill
1.3	28.3	R	**Tempe Wick Rd.** (T). Road you were on has changed name to Leddell Rd.
0.7	29.0	L	Into **Morristown National Historic Park**
0.3	29.3		**Visitor's Center Parking Lot.** End of route

ROCKAWAY VALLEY — 33.1 MILES

This is a traditional Morris Area Freewheeler route that was used to reawaken the cycling muscles after a winter of non-riding. Now you see many racers working out on the roads of the Rockaway Valley, and many hardy winter riders as well!

Terrain: Varies from gently rolling to a "bit hilly." Portions right near the Rockaway River are flat.
Traffic: Light to moderate, except busy on Rt. 511 and near Denville and Boonton.
Road Conditions: Excellent! Hats off to the local road departments for making the roads of this route (for the most part) very smooth.
Points of Interest: Old homes and farms of the **Rockaway Valley**; **Silas Condict County Park** (hiking, picnicking, paddleboating); **Pyramid Mountain Nature Center**; **Grace Lord Park** (gorge of the Rockaway River).

The **Rockaway Valley** is a long, narrow corridor of lightly developed wetlands that has retained its cycling appeal despite its location near the center of Morris County. The recent opening of I-287 has actually led to a decrease in traffic along its main north-south roads. The scenery is still beautiful: Lakes and ponds abound, and tree-covered hills are always on the horizon.

Besides being a favorite area for bike racers (probably because of the long distances between turns), the valley is good for beginning bike tourists and intermediates who like to stop along the way and see the sights. Two short hikes are noted: one to a viewpoint overlooking hills and lakes and another to a large waterfall. Longer hikes are possible at Pyramid Mountain.

Ride out of Denville, a busy Morris County town that was once a Morris Canal port. Soon you'll be in the Rockaway Valley. Watch for historic plaques that explain the significance of several of the 18th-Century stone homes. One was owned by a Quaker who was the first slave-owner in Morris County to free his slaves.

The detour into the hills west of Rockaway Valley Rd. is worthwhile for the quiet slopeside horse farms and views. Plus you'll have a great 1-mile descent on Split Rock Rd.

Head north to Silas Condict Park, where you can get off your bike and walk to a beautiful overlook. Then ride through the pretty Fayson Lakes. A small store is available here for snacks and drinks.

Return south along Rt. 511, which parallels the Boonton Reservoirs. Look for a pair of swans in each lake. Past the reservoir is Pyramid Mountain Nature Center, which is "headquarters" for miles of rugged hiking trails in the hills on either side of Rt. 511. Tripod Rock, a unique formation, is reachable by an hour's round-trip walk.

In Boonton, the route takes you alongside a clearly visible section of the Morris Canal, once a busy waterway carrying local iron to the foundries but closed since 1924. Also in Boonton, be sure to walk into Grace Lord Park. The Rockaway River cuts an impressive gorge through town, and includes a major waterfall.

Cycle back to Denville via the Boulevard, the main road of the wealthy old suburb of Mountain Lakes. The jog on the map back north into the Rockaway Valley covers some very flat, pretty roads that pass a farmstand, and also passes E.C. Peer's, a store/restaurant that has been in business since Morris Canal days.

Directions to Starting Point: The **A&P Shopping Center in Denville** is located on Rt. 53, just south of Rt. 46. From I-80, use Exit 39 westbound, Exit 38 eastbound. Both exits put you on Rt. 46 eastbound. Turn off at the ramp for Rt. 53 south, then go just past the first light. The shopping center is on the right.

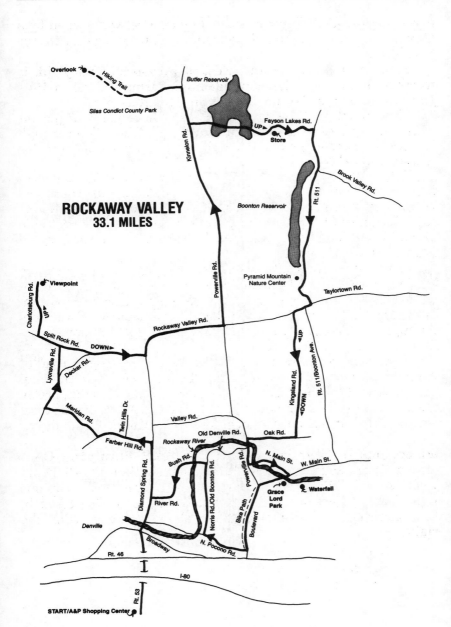

ROCKAWAY VALLEY
33.1 MILES

Overlook

Hiking Trail

Butler Reservoir

Silas Condict County Park

Fayson Lakes Rd.

UP

Store

Kinnelon Rd.

Boonton Reservoir

Brook Valley Rd.

Rt. 511

Charlotteburg Rd.

Viewpoint

UP

Powerville Rd.

Pyramid Mountain Nature Center

Taylortown Rd.

Split Rock Rd.

DOWN

Rockaway Valley Rd.

Lyonsville Rd.

Decker Rd.

Kingland Rd.

Rt. 511/Boonton Ave.

UP

DOWN

Meriden Rd.

Twin Hills Dr.

Valley Rd.

Old Denville Rd.

Oak Rd.

Farber Hill Rd.

Rockaway River

N. Main St.

W. Main St.

Bush Rd.

Powerville Rd.

Grace Lord Park

Waterfall

Diamond Spring Rd.

River Rd.

Norris Rd./Old Boonton Rd.

Bike Path

Boulevard

Denville

Broadway

N. Pocono Rd.

Rt. 46

I-80

Rt. 53

START/A&P Shopping Center

PT.-PT.	CUME	DIRECTION	STREET/LANDMARK
0.0	0.0	**L**	Exit the A&P shopping center onto **Rt. 53 North**. Go under I-80 and Rt. 46 and straight at first traffic light
0.3	0.3	**BR**	At five-way traffic light in center of Denville onto **Diamond Spring Rd.** This road will eventually change name to **Rockaway Valley Rd.**
3.2	3.5	**L**	**Farber Hill Rd.**
0.6	4.1	**R**	**Meriden Rd.** (possibly no street sign). This is the second right turn (the first right turn is Twin Hills Dr.)
1.0	5.1	**R**	**Lyonsville Rd.** (yield sign)
0.3	5.4	**BL**	At fork, to continue on **Lyonsville Rd.** (Decker Rd. goes right)
1.0	6.4	**L**	**Split Rock Rd.** (T)
0.4	6.8	**R**	**Charlotteburg Rd.**
0.2	7.0		Ride until pavement ends, then **U-Turn** and return the way you came. Enjoy grand view from top of field in horse farm!
0.2	7.2	**L**	**Split Rock Rd.** (T)
1.7	8.9	**SL**	**Rockaway Valley Rd.** (T)
0.8	9.7	**L**	**Powerville Rd.** (stop sign). *CAUTION: cars coming from the right are not visible until the last moment.* Road will change name to **Kinnelon Rd.**
5.1	14.8	**L**	Into **Silas Condict County Park**. Turn is 0.2 miles past Kinnelon High School (on right)

PT.-PT.	CUME	DIRECTION	STREET/LANDMARK
0.9	15.7		At end of parking lot, you might wish to lock your bike and take a ten-minute walk to Overlook (correct trail has sign for Overlook). Then **U-Turn** and return out of park the way you came in
0.9	16.6	R	**Kinnelon Rd.** (T)
1.0	17.6	L	**Fayson Lakes Rd.** (turn is just before a "Speed Limit 35" sign)
1.0	18.6		**Store** on right
1.1	19.7	R	**Rt. 511** toward Boonton (T)
2.2	21.9		**Pyramid Mountain Nature Center** on right
0.5	22.4	R	**Taylortown Rd.** (yield sign). Do not turn immediately left to continue on Rt. 511, rather continue straight on **Taylortown Rd.**
0.3	22.7	L	**Kingsland Rd.** (blue aboveground swimming pool on corner)
1.7	24.4	R	**Oak Rd.** (T)
0.4	24.8	L	**Powerville Rd.** (T)
0.4	25.2	L	**North Main St.** toward Boonton. Sign may be hidden behind trees. Cross Rockaway River immediately
0.6	25.8		**Morris Canal** visible on right
0.2	26.0	R	**West Main St.** (T; no street sign). Cross Rockaway River
0.1	26.1		**Grace Lord Park** on left (with gazebo). Walk about 0.2 miles into park along river to view waterfall and gorge

PT.-PT.	CUME	DIRECTION	STREET/LANDMARK
0.5	26.6		Road changes name to **Boulevard** as you **curve left** to enter Mountain Lakes. You may wish to use the bike path, which parallels the road on the right
2.0	28.6	**R**	**North Pocono Rd.** (traffic light)
0.7	29.3	**R**	**Norris Rd./Old Boonton Rd.** (toward Rockaway River Country Club). Turn is in the midst of a downhill
1.3	30.6	**L**	**Bush Rd.** (sign may be hidden under a tree). Road changes name to **River Rd.**
1.0	31.6	**L**	**Diamond Spring Rd.** (T; no street sign). **E.C. Peer** store and restaurant on left shortly after turn
1.2	32.8	**BL**	At five-way traffic light in center of Denville onto **Rt. 53 South/ East Main St.**
0.3	33.1	**R**	Into **A&P Shopping Center.** End of route

RIDES STARTING IN SUSSEX COUNTY

A big county in the northwestern corner of New Jersey, Sussex is growing due to its proximity to busy Morris County, but it is as yet in no danger of developing as did Morris. Agriculture is still important here, and that means on many routes cyclists will see more cows than cars.

Besides lovely roads on rolling hills featuring grand views of woods and corn, Sussex includes attractions such as High Point State Park, Stokes State Forest, Franklin Mineral Museum, Stirling Mine Tour, Space Farms Zoo and Museum, and a sizeable section of the Delaware River, free-flowing, clean and very refreshing on a hot day.

Andover-Franklin explores Sussex's past as a mining area, passing Stirling Mine Tour enroute to the Franklin Mineral Museum. On the mine tour, visitors can descend into an old zinc mine, while at the museum guests can actually "mine" the glowing rocks that indicate the presence of zinc. You will marvel when the lights are turned out in the phosphorescent mineral room and the long-wave lamps go on. The colors are amazing as these rocks "glow in the dark." Besides the museum, the route features nice riding near woodsy and hilly Lake Mohawk.

Andover-Swartswood Lake is a rerouting of a route from the previous edition that started in Warren County's Allamuchy School. It features the flat Tranquility Valley, true to its name with acres of cornfields, then rolling hills to Swartswood Lake with its state park, swimming beach and several quiet picnic spots.

Ross's Corner-Wantage heads north toward the borough of Sussex through still more pretty farm country. Among the features are Space Farms Zoo and Museum with its large animal collection, Sussex Airport (home of a great air show in August) and the antiquing village of Lafayette.

Sunrise Mountain-High Point starts in Stokes State Forest on a road designed to provide motorists scenic views—and cyclists a good challenge! Stop for a swim at Lake Marcia under the High Point monument, then return to the starting point by riding through the pretty farm country under the Kittatinny Ridge.

Sussex-Wantage features Wantage Township, a mostly rural area where the cyclist can take photos of enormous dairy herds grazing in huge green fields with the mountains in the distance. Rolling hills take the rider to the shoulder of the ridge; the reward is a tremendous zoom of a downhill. Ambitious cyclists can combine this route with **Sunrise Mountain-High Point** for a hilly metric century.

Upper Delaware Water Gap concentrates on the sparsely-travelled roads in the northwest corner of the state. The ride starts on the west side of the Kittatinny Ridge, so there is little major hill climbing. Visit Dingman's Falls in Pennsylvania on this ride, as well as Peter's Valley Craft Village.

ANDOVER-FRANKLIN—29.5 MILES

This Sussex County route has been modified from the previous edition of RIDE GUIDE *to include Sussex County's newest attraction, the Stirling Mine Tour.*

Terrain: Moderately rolling to downright hilly into Sparta, rolling to level thereafter.
Traffic: Mostly very light to moderate, except a little busy near and north of Sparta and in Franklin.
Road Conditions: Good, but local road departments often spread gravel on back roads so watch for it.
Points of Interest: Sparta (a pretty town on picturesque Lake Mohawk); **Stirling Mine Tour**; **Franklin Mineral Museum**; beautiful backroads cycling in Sussex County.

Rock hounds will be especially pleased by this route, which heads north to the Franklin Mineral Museum, home of one of the world's largest displays of "glowing rocks" and a do-it-yourself quarry where you can "mine" your own phosphorescent minerals.

The mineral museum includes a room where the show begins when the lights go out and a special long-wave light is pointed toward a wall of ordinary-looking rocks. Then all sorts of greens, oranges, and violets jump out at you in an amazing display of one of nature's surprises. The Franklin area was a major zinc-producing area until very recently, and miners used low-wave lamps to detect deposits of zinc and other "glowing" minerals.

Even if you're not especially interested in minerals and mining, you will enjoy this pleasant meander through some of Sussex County's finest back roads. Head north out of Andover toward Sparta. The worst hills of the whole ride are in the first seven miles as you roller coaster your way to Lake Mohawk.

The lake is a beautiful sight, especially in the fall. For some reason, the air seems crisper and cleaner around Lake Mohawk.

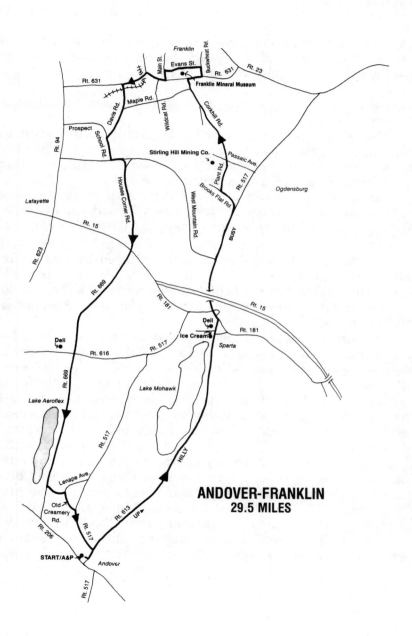

ANDOVER-FRANKLIN
29.5 MILES

At the northern end of the lake is Sparta, with a pretty two-block downtown (deli and possibly ice cream available). Just off the main street, look for a boardwalk behind the stores overlooking the lake, a good place to rest and take a picture.

Next head north out of Sparta toward Ogdensburg and the Stirling Mine Tour. Even if you don't take the tour, the giant structures of this old zinc mine are interesting to look at. Rest rooms and a gift shop are available. Bring a jacket for the tour—it's cold underground.

A few miles further of relatively flat pedaling take you to Franklin and the mineral museum, the halfway point on the ride.

Then cycle south on beautiful Houses Corner Road, where open fields and 10-mile views are the rule. On Rt. 669 you will enjoy level to downhill riding all the way back into Andover. The one exception to the pretty rural scenery, the huge limestone quarry, is unique in its own way with a half-mile stretch of shiny limestone piled along the side of the road.

Directions to Starting Point: The **Andover A&P** is at the junctions of Route 206 and 517 in Andover, about 7 miles north of I-80 Exit 25, on the right.

PT.-PT.	CUME	DIRECTION	STREET/LANDMARK
0.0	0.0	**L**	Exit south end of A&P parking lot onto **Rt. 517 North**
0.1	0.1	**S**	**Rt. 613/Mohawk Rd.** (stop sign). Rt. 517 goes left
0.4	0.5	**L**	Curve left to continue on **Rt. 613**. Roseville Rd. goes right
6.6	7.1		Entering downtown **Sparta** (**stores** on left). Continue straight past downtown Sparta
0.2	7.3	**L**	**Rt. 181 North** (T). After making turn, do not go into jug handle to continue on Rt. 181, but go straight

PT.-PT.	CUME	DIRECTION	STREET/LANDMARK
			ahead toward the traffic light and toward Park & Ride/Sparta Township
0.2	7.5	S	At traffic light onto **Rt. 517 North**. *CAUTION: Busy road*
3.3	10.8	L	**Brooks Flat Rd.** (toward Stirling Mine Tour)
0.4	11.2	R	**Plant Rd.** (follow mine tour signs)
0.8	12.0	L	**Passaic Ave.**
0.1	12.1	L	Into **Stirling Hill Mining Co.** After visiting, return to **Passaic Ave.** and turn **right**
0.1	12.3	L	**Cork Hill Rd.** Ride through long, dark one-lane tunnel
2.0	14.3	R	**Franklin Ave./Rt. 631**
0.1	14.4	L	Toward **Franklin Mineral Museum** onto unmarked **Buckwheat Rd.**
0.2	14.6	L	**Evans St.**, toward Franklin Mineral Museum
0.1	14.7		**Franklin Mineral Museum** on left
0.3	15.0	L	**Main St.** (stop sign)
0.0	15.0	R	**Church St./Rt. 631** (T)
0.3	15.3	L	At fork, to continue on **Rt. 631**
0.4	15.7	L	**Davis Rd.** Road crosses railroad tracks immediately
2.3	18.0	L	**Prospect School Rd.** (T)
0.4	18.4	L	**West Mountain Rd.** (T)
0.1	18.5	R	**Houses Corner Rd.**
2.6	21.1	S	Cross Rt. 15/Lafayette Rd. to continue on **Houses Corner Rd./Rt. 669**. *CAUTION: dangerous intersection*

PT.-PT.	CUME	DIRECTION	STREET/LANDMARK
1.8	22.9	S	Cross Rt. 616 at traffic light to continue on **Rt. 669**. **Deli** on Rt. 616 a few hundred feet to the right of this intersection
5.3	28.2	L	**Old Creamery Rd.**
0.4	28.6	R	At T to continue on **Old Creamery Rd.** Lenape Ave. goes left
0.3	28.9	R	**Rt. 517 South/Lenape Rd.** (T)
0.5	29.4	R	At stop sign to continue on **Rt. 517 South**. Mohawk Rd. goes left
0.1	29.5	R	Into **A&P Shopping Center**. End of route

ANDOVER-SWARTSWOOD LAKE—41.3 MILES

This route is similar to Allamuchy-Swartswood Lake in the previous edition of RIDE GUIDE. The closing of the Allamuchy School parking lot on weekends necessitated the relocating of the starting point to Andover, adding three miles to the route.

Terrain: Gently rolling to Swartswood Lake, then hilly returning to Tranquility Valley, followed by gently rolling once back in the valley.

Traffic: Very light to occasionally moderate near Swartswood State Park.

Road Conditions: Excellent. Smoothly paved roads, except for a brief bumpy stretch on Fredon-Springdale Rd.

Points of Interest: Johnsonburg and **Stillwater** (some interesting old buildings); **Swartswood State Park** (swimming, picnicking); **Keen's Mill** (a good lunch spot by a 19th Century stone mill); beautiful cycling through quiet rural roads of Sussex and Warren counties.

Explore the beauty of the Tranquility Valley and the area around Swartswood Lake in this 41-mile loop. Quiet roads, views of farms, lakes and fields all start immediately after leaving Andover, a pleasant town with several antique shops and restaurants. Several interesting little hamlets, including Johnsonburg (look for some old buildings, including one that served as a "gaol"—jail—in pre-Revolutionary times) and Stillwater make this an excellent sojourn, without too many awful hills.

Good lunch spots on this route include the fishing/boating access to Little Swartswood Lake and Keen's Mill, and an old stone mill on the west shore of Swartswood. Look for the date 1835 etched into the stone wall. Or you might wish to stop in Stillwater alongside the babbling brook next to the pretty Inn at Stillwater.

The return route does present one major challenge in the form of Phil Hardin Rd., which is one of the steepest climbs in

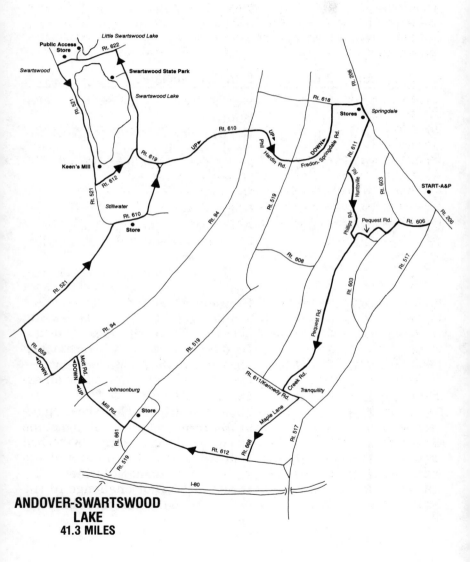

**ANDOVER-SWARTSWOOD
LAKE
41.3 MILES**

RIDE GUIDE. The huffin' and puffin' is short-lived, however, and riders enjoy downhill to rolling terrain thereafter.

Directions to Starting Point: The **Andover A&P** is just north of the junctions of Route 206 and 517 in Andover, about 7 miles north of I-80 Exit 25, on the right.

PT.-PT.	CUME	DIRECTION	STREET/LANDMARK
0.0	0.0	L	Exit shopping center onto **Rt. 206 South**
0.2	0.2	R	**Rt. 517 South/Brighton Ave.**, toward Tranquility and Hackettstown
0.2	0.4	R	Just beyond traffic light, onto **Rt. 606 West/Brighton Ave.**
1.1	1.5	L	**Rt. 603 South**
0.5	2.0	R	**Pequest Rd.**
0.3	2.3	R	At unmarked T at bottom of hill
0.3	2.6	S	Continue on **Pequest Rd.** Phillips Rd. goes off to right
0.6	3.2	S	Go through tunnel under former railroad
1.5	4.7	L	**Kennedy Rd./Rt. 611** (T)
1.4	6.1	R	**Maple Lane**. Cemetery on left just after turn. Road will become **County Rt. 668** upon entering Warren County
1.5	7.6	R	**Rt. 612 North** toward Johnsonburg (T)
3.5	11.1	S	Cross Rt. 519 at stop sign
0.2	11.3	L	**Rt. 661 South** (T). Note: Turn **right** at this corner and proceed one-tenth of a mile for a **store** (on right)
0.2	11.5	R	**Mill Rd.**
0.7	12.2	S	At stop sign, onto unmarked **Mott Rd.**
1.3	13.5	L	**Rt. 94** (T). *CAUTION: Steep hill before this intersection. Control your speed!*

PT.-PT.	CUME	DIRECTION	STREET/LANDMARK
0.8	14.3	R	**County Rt. 659**, toward Stillwater
1.2	15.5	R	**Rt. 521 North** (stop sign)
3.6	19.1	R	**Rt. 610** (T). Rt. 521 goes left
0.1	19.2		**Store** on right
0.2	19.4	L	Curve left after bridge to continue on **Rt. 610** toward Newton
1.7	21.1	L	At fork, onto **Rt. 619**
3.0	24.1		Entrance to **Swartswood State Park** (swimming, picnicking, bathrooms) on left
0.7	24.8	L	**Rt. 622** (T)
0.4	25.2		Entrance to **Little Swartswood Lake Public Access** (quieter picnic spot) on right
0.5	25.7		**Store** on right
0.1	25.8	L	**Rt. 521 South** (T), toward Middleville and Stillwater
2.5	28.3		**Keen's Mill** on left; another good picnic spot
0.5	28.8	L	**Rt. 612** (toward Newton and Fredon)
0.8	29.6	R	**Rt. 619** (T)
0.6	30.2	BL	At Y onto **Rt. 610**
2.0	32.2	S	Cross Rt. 94 toward Springdale onto **Phil Hardin Rd.** Steep ascent ahead!
1.1	33.3	S	Cross Rt. 519 onto **Fredon-Springdale Rd.** *CAUTION: winding, steep descent*
1.1	34.4	R	**Rt. 618** (T)
1.3	35.7	R	**Rt. 206** (T). Two **stores** on right after turn
0.1	35.8	R	**Rt. 611**, toward Greendell and Tranquility
0.7	36.5	L	**Huntsville Rd.** Road changes name to Phillips Rd.

PT.-PT.	CUME	DIRECTION	STREET/LANDMARK
2.0	38.5	S	Continue on **Phillips Rd.** where Macklerey Rd. comes off to the right
0.2	38.7	L	**Pequest Rd.** (T)
0.3	39.0	L	At stone wall after curve to continue on **Pequest Rd.**
0.3	39.3	L	**Rt. 603 North** (T)
0.5	39.8	R	**Rt. 606** (T)
1.1	40.9	L	**Rt. 517 North** (traffic light)
0.2	41.1	L	**Rt. 206 North** (T)
0.2	41.3	R	Into **A&P Shopping Center**. End of route

ROSS'S CORNER-WANTAGE—38.2 MILES

A two-wheeled visit to the Sussex Air Show inspired this ride. The countryside surrounding the Sussex Airport is rural, rolling, and beckons exploration. The new attraction for the area is a minor league baseball stadium, which will be just north of the starting point. Check out a game after the ride!

Terrain: Undulating, with gradual climbs and long descents. A few shorter, steeper hills as well.
Traffic: Light to moderate, with busier traffic near the borough of Sussex and on a short stretch of Rt. 23.
Road Conditions: Very smooth, for the most part. One small stretch of dirt road near the end of the ride.
Points of Interest: New Jersey Cardinals stadium; **Space Farms Zoo and Museum**; **Sussex Airport** (air show in August); **Lafayette** antique stores; beautiful backroads cycling in rural Sussex County.

Wantage Township, which follows the valley of the Wallkill River, lies within sight of the larger hills of Vernon Township to the east (famous for ski resorts) and the Kittatinny Ridge to the west. Thus the cyclist has the pleasure of mountain scenery without climbing.

This ride is not flat, but rather pleasantly undulating. The hills are long and gradual for the most part, and feature wide panoramas of fields, dairy farms, and the mountains in the distance.

Start by heading north out of Ross's Corner and immediately into farm country. Although there are occasional single-family-home developments, this area of Sussex is still predominantly rural.

Visit Space Farms Zoo and Museum, which opens 9 a.m. daily May through October. Owned and operated by the Space family for over 60 years, the zoo is the largest private collection of North American wild animals. The star attraction is a one-

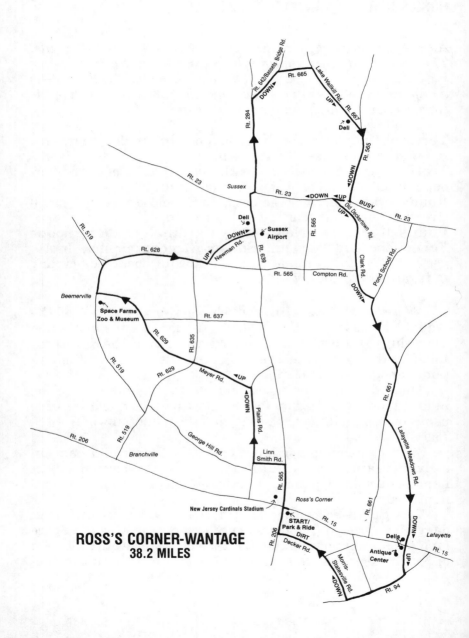

ROSS'S CORNER-WANTAGE
38.2 MILES

ton bear named Goliath. Space Farms also features an auto museum, Americana exhibit, toys, firearms, clocks, and other collections.

Next, cycle to Sussex Airport. If you're here at air-show time (approximately third weekend in August) you'll be thankful you're on only two wheels, as auto traffic gets clogged for miles. Sussex is home base for several air stunt champions, so you can expect a great show.

Head north through the borough of Sussex into Wantage Township. Route 284 is rolling, then expect a grand descent down to the Wallkill River on Route 642. Cross the river and encounter a long, gradual climb.

Old Deckertown Road, off of Rt. 23, seems to have a lot of snarling, nasty dogs, all of which seem to be tied up, fortunately. The ride south goes up and down gently, passing more cows and corn, a relaxing route on roads with little traffic.

If you can hold off on lunch until Lafayette, you will find a pretty picnic grove by a stream next to the antique center south of Route 15. The shops here are worth exploring.

Soon you'll be on the one dirt road of the trip, and then back to Ross's Corner. The contrast between the quiet Sussex and the busy, growing Sussex of the highways at Ross's Corner is remarkable.

Directions to Starting Point: Ross's Corner Park & Ride is located at the northern end of Rt. 15, where it meets Rt. 206. It is about 18 miles north of I-80 Exit 34B on Rt. 15 or 8 miles north of Newton on Rt. 206.

PT.-PT.	CUME	DIRECTION	STREET/LANDMARK
0.0	0.0	**L**	Exit park & ride onto **Rt. 15 North**
0.0	0.0	**R**	Immediate right turn at traffic light onto **Rt. 565 North. Baseball stadium** will be on left
1.4	1.4	**L**	**Linn Smith Rd.**

PT.-PT.	CUME	DIRECTION	STREET/LANDMARK
0.6	2.0	**R**	**Plains Rd.** (T)
1.7	3.7	**L**	**Meyer Rd.** Climb a short, steep hill immediately after turn
1.1	4.8	**S**	Onto **Rt. 629**. Rt. 635 goes right
2.9	7.7	**R**	**Rt. 519 North** (T). To visit **Space Farms Zoo & Museum**, turn **left** here. Entrance is 0.1 miles on left
1.3	9.0	**BR**	At fork, onto **Rt. 628**. Rt. 519 goes left
2.1	11.1	**L**	**Newman Rd.** Turn is just after pretty gorge (on right)
1.0	12.1	**L**	**Rt. 639** (T). **Sussex Airport** is straight ahead of you at this intersection. Enter here during the air show. To visit at other times, turn **right** at this intersection for the airport's main entrance
0.2	12.3		**Deli** on left
0.6	12.9	**S**	Onto **Rt. 23 South** at traffic light
0.1	13.0	**R**	To continue on **Rt. 23 South**
0.0	13.0	**L**	Immediate **left** at traffic light onto **Rt. 284 North**
4.0	17.0	**R**	Rt. 642/Bassets Bridge Rd.
1.1	18.1	**R**	**Rt. 665**. Turn is just past bridge over Wallkill River
0.7	18.8	**R**	**Lake Wallkill Rd.** (T; no street sign). Becomes **Rt. 667**
2.9	21.7		**Deli** on right
0.3	22.0	**R**	**Rt. 565 South**
2.5	24.5	**R**	**Rt. 23 North** (T). *CAUTION: Busy road—use shoulder*

PT.-PT.	CUME	DIRECTION	STREET/LANDMARK
0.4	24.9	**SL**	**Old Deckertown Rd.** (unmarked). Turn is at the top of the hill, by Sussex Redi-Mix, onto a small, narrow road that goes uphill and soon passes a cemetery on the left. Do not go down the next hill on Rt. 23!
0.7	25.6	**R**	Curve right onto **Clark Rd.**
1.1	26.7	**R**	**Pond School Rd.** (T; no signs)
2.3	29.0	**R**	**Rt. 661** (T)
2.2	31.2	**L**	**Lafayette Meadows Rd.** No street sign! Turn is before a cattle crossing sign and opposite a yellow house with a two-story porch. "Weight Limit 4 Tons" sign on the right after the turn
2.9	34.1	**S**	At stop sign onto **Rt. 659**, crossing Rt. 15. **Delis** on right before and after the intersection. **Antique Center** with streamside picnic area on right after intersection
0.4	34.5	**BR**	**Rt. 94 South** (yield sign)
1.1	35.6	**R**	**Morris-Statesville Rd.** (unmarked). Second right turn off Rt. 94. Road is opposite United Telephone of New Jersey Service Center
1.1	36.7	**L**	At unmarked fork. Road becomes dirt
1.0	37.7	**R**	At stop sign onto unmarked **Rt. 206 North**
0.5	38.2	**R**	**Rt. 15 South** (traffic light). Then immediate **right** into **Ross's Corner Park & Ride**, end of route

SUNRISE MOUNTAIN-HIGH POINT—32.5 MILES

The highest roads in the state of New Jersey are explored on this new RIDE GUIDE *route. But don't let that distinction bother you. Take it slow and you will enjoy tremendous views without overtaxing your "engine"!*

Terrain: Heading north to High Point, you will experience some of the steepest ups and downs in the state. The hills are longer and somewhat gentler for the first 9.5 miles within Stokes State Forest, then shorter and much steeper in High Point State Park. The southbound return is much easier on the legs, heading through rolling valley farm country, until the final two-mile ascent back to the starting point on the Kittatinny Ridge.

Traffic: Extremely light through Stokes and High Point, even on busy summer and fall weekends. Very light on the return outside the park, except moderate on Rt. 23.

Road Conditions: Excellent throughout, except bumpy on the one stretch you need a smooth road—the incredibly steep descent on Rt. 23.

Points of Interest: The forest and views of the **Sunrise Mountain** section of **Stokes State Forest**; **High Point Park** (monument and **swimming** at Lake Marcia); pretty rolling farm country on the return route (bring your camera); **Space Farms Zoo & Museum**.

Why would one willingly ride a bicycle up some of the steepest hills in the state to the highest point in the state? Not because "it is there" (although that was the author's reason for exploring this route!), but because as a cyclist you have the option to stop when you are tired, catch your breath, and take as much time as you need to complete the 32.5 hilly miles of this route.

Stokes State Forest, through which you ride for the first 9.5 miles, is a large wilderness area and home to much of the Garden State's 50 or so wild bears. If you are riding through the woods here at a quiet time in late spring, you might just spot one. If not, keep an eye out for other plentiful wildlife — wild turkeys, bobcats, foxes, and white tail deer, to name a few.

Sunrise Mountain Road, recently designated one-way northbound, is a smooth surface and relatively free of cars even on the busiest weekends. Start climbing only a half-mile out of the parking lot, but at 3.5 miles get the camera ready—a beautiful view opens up on the left side of the road.

The climb up to the actual Sunrise Mountain overlook is a side road coming off to the right. Park and lock your bike at the top and stroll down the famous Appalachian Trail about 50 feet to enjoy a panorama of the farm valley to the East.

Now it's time to enjoy close to five miles of almost continuous downhill, a good reward for the effort put in so far. Unfortunately, upon exiting Stokes into High Point State Park, the cyclist encounters a number of roller-coaster ups and downs much steeper (but fortunately shorter) than those experienced in Stokes.

Sawmill Road is a particularly beautiful road with practically no traffic, heading past a number of swamps and lakes where one can stop and view birds, turtles and frogs. Eventually the road ends and the final big climb into the main part of High Point State Park begins. The reward is a refreshing swim at Lake Marcia, one of the nicest and cleanest lakes in the State Park system. The adventurous might wish to continue one mile past the lake to the monument, stake their claim to having pedaled to the top of New Jersey, then return down to the lake.

Return via the farm valley east of the Kittatinny Ridge. Check brakes before going down the incredibly steep section of Rt. 23, and stop for food at Colesville Deli or eat delicious pies at Elias Cole Restaurant. Rts. 519 and 649 are typically stunning Sussex County farm roads, with cows and corn at every corner.

Alas, most of the last two miles feature a climb back up to the ridge and your car, but at least there is a 1/2-mile descent to victory and the end of the route.

Cyclists who wish a longer route can link this route at the Colesville Deli with **Sussex-Wantage**. See page 105.

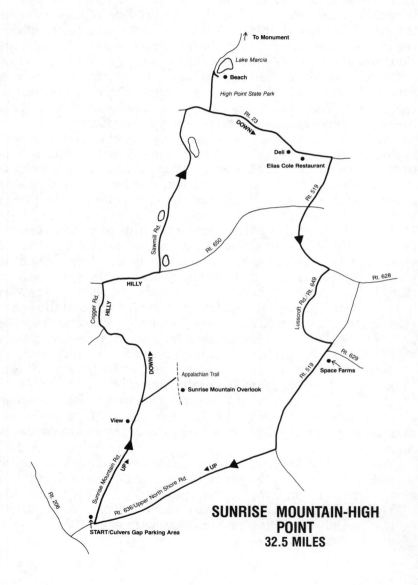

↑ To Monument

Lake Marcia

● Beach

High Point State Park

Rt. 23

DOWN▲

Deli ●
●
Elias Cole Restaurant

Rt. 519

Sawmill Rd.

Rt. 650

Rt. 628

HILLY

Crigger Rd.

HILLY

Lusscroft Rd./Rt. 649

DOWN

Appalachian Trail

● Sunrise Mountain Overlook

View ●

Rt. 629

●
Space Farms

Rt. 519

Sunrise Mountain Rd.

UP ▲

◄UP

UP▲

Rt. 206

Rt. 636/Upper North Shore Rd.

●
START/Culvers Gap Parking Area

SUNRISE MOUNTAIN-HIGH POINT
32.5 MILES

Directions to Starting Point: The route begins in the **Culvers Gap Parking Area** in Stokes State Forest. From Ross's Corners, the junction of Routes 15 and 206 (18 miles north of I-80 Exit 34B), continue north on Rt. 206 for 6.2 miles, then turn right on Rt. 636 (sign points toward Sunrise Mountain). Turn left in 0.2 miles onto Sunrise Mountain Scenic Road, and make a quick left into the parking area.

PT.-PT.	CUME	DIRECTION	STREET/LANDMARK
0.0	0.0	L	**Sunrise Mountain Rd.**
3.2	3.2		Tremendous **view** on left side of road
0.8	4.0	R	At fork, toward **Sunrise Mountain Scenic Overlook**
0.8	4.8		Park and lock bike at parking lot and walk a few steps south on the Appalachian Trail to enjoy tremendous view to the east from top of Sunrise Mountain. Then return down the way you came up
0.7	5.5	SR	To continue north on **Sunrise Mountain Rd.** *CAUTION: In one mile, watch speed on several steep, curvy descents*
3.0	8.5	S	**Crigger Rd.** (road toward Stokes State Forest office goes off to left). Climb series of ascents and descents even steeper than Sunrise Mountain Rd.!
1.0	9.5	R	**Rt. 655 East** (T)—more serious ups & downs. By now you are cursing the author but it's a nice ride, admit it
1.8	11.3	L	**Sawmill Rd.** (toward "Office" and "Monument"). Turn is after causeway over swamp

PT.-PT.	CUME	DIRECTION	STREET/LANDMARK
4.4	15.7	**R**	**Rt. 23 South** (T) toward park office. Horrendous uphill
0.4	16.1	**L**	Into **High Point Park**
0.6	16.7	**R**	Into parking lot for **Lake Marcia** and **beach** (optional—cycle an additional uphill one mile—the last few hundred yards of which are very steep—to reach tower, then return to lake). After stop at beach and lake, return to park road and turn **left** to exit park
0.6	17.3	**L**	**Rt. 23 South** (T). Prepare for incredibly steep and bumpy downhill—check brakes before you launch!
2.6	19.9		**Colesville Deli** on right—**Elias Cole restaurant** for pies on right in additional 0.2 miles—only food stops. *Link at deli to Sussex-Wantage route, mile 14.9, page 108*
0.7	20.6	**R**	**Rt. 519 South.** Gas station on corner, and sign for Space Farms. Short, steep climb immediately after turn
1.6	22.2	**S**	At stop sign to continue on **Rt. 519 South**. Cross Rt. 650
1.9	24.1	**R**	**Lusscroft Rd./Rt. 649 South**
1.7	25.8	**R**	**Rt. 519 South** (T)
0.2	26.0		**Space Farms** on left
3.4	29.4	**R**	**Upper North Shore Rd./Rt. 636**. Two miles of climbs
3.1	32.5	**SR**	**Sunrise Mountain Rd.** (turn is after first significant downhill in awhile)
0.0	32.5	**L**	Immediate left into **Culvers Gap Parking Area**. End of route

SUSSEX-WANTAGE—29.8 MILES

Wantage Township, a vast expanse of farmland between two mountain ridges, warrants a second route. The long drive to Sussex is worth it when you check out the views available from your handlebars here!

Terrain: Roller-coaster, tending toward uphill when headed north and west (beginning of route) and downhill on the south and east return. One two-mile stretch of flat! (Clove Rd.)
Traffic: Practically non-existent on the quiet unnumbered roads that make up the majority of this route. Otherwise, light.
Road Conditions: Mostly smooth, occasionally choppy. A little over a mile of hard-packed unpaved road near the end of the ride (parallel paved route available).
Points of Interest: Cows and views! **Colesville Deli** at middle of route

The **northwest corner** of Sussex County is still the domain of the dairy farm. Chances are very good that cows will outnumber people three-to-one as you cycle along the ups and downs of Wantage Township's back roads. Views of the Kittatinny Ridge to the west, and the High Point Monument on top, are astounding.

Start by heading north into the roller-coaster workout of Lower Unionville Rd. This sort of quadriceps-stressing cadence continues for many miles. When Wolfpit Rd. is reached, prepare for a sudden glimpse of the High Point obelisk as a tremendous downhill appears under the front wheel. Watch for the unmarked, un-stop-signed intersection of Quarry Rd. while zipping down the hill.

After passing numerous large dairy herds, reach the corner of Unionville Rd. at the very top of a switchback downhill. Good news—the route turns left, down the hill. Then comes the only truly flat part of the ride, Clove Rd.

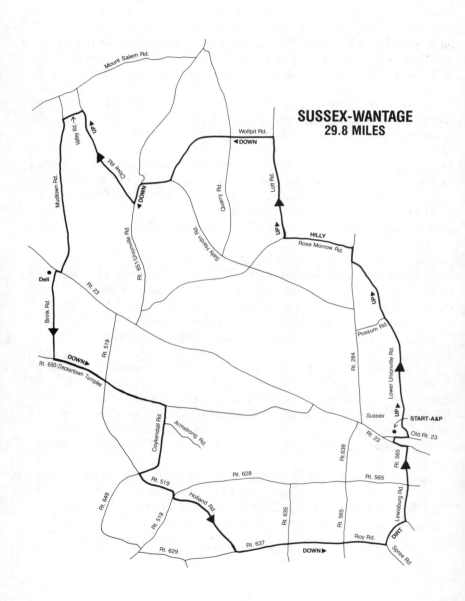

SUSSEX-WANTAGE
29.8 MILES

Soon the course heads south along the shoulder of the Kittatinny Ridge, with more great views both west and east. Stop for some food at the Colesville Store then continue south. The prevailing direction is downhill when the compass points east, and Rt. 650 and 637 contain some impressive descents.

Near the end, slow down and enjoy a mile of hard-packed dirt road. The surface is smooth enough for most skinny-tired bikes, but Rt. 565 provides a paved alternate.

Ambitious cyclists can combine **Sussex-Wantage** with **Sunrise Mountain-High Point** (page 100) for a 62.3-mile hilly metric century.

Directions to Starting Point: The **A&P Shopping Center** is on the right side of Rt. 23 northbound, before the borough of Sussex, about 4 miles north of the junction of Rt. 94 in Hamburg, 26 miles north of the junction of I-287 and Rt. 23, and 34 miles north of Exit 53 of I-80 Westbound.

PT.-PT.	CUME	DIRECTION	STREET/LANDMARK
0.0	0.0	L	Exit shopping center onto **Old Rt. 23**
0.1	0.1	L	**Lower Unionville Rd.**
0.1	0.2	BR	At unmarked fork, to continue on **Lower Unionville Rd.**
3.8	4.0	R	**Rt. 284** (T; no street sign)
0.2	4.2	L	**Rose Morrow Rd.**, toward Quarryville
0.9	5.1	R	**Lott Rd.**
1.6	6.7	L	**Wolfpit Rd.**
0.7	7.4	S	*CAUTION! While cycling very fast down hill, you will encounter the intersection of Quarry Rd. There are no stop signs on either road, so approach with care!*
1.4	8.8	BR	At intersection with Sally Hardin Rd., to continue on **Wolfpit Rd.**
0.4	9.2	L	**Rt. 651 South/Unionville Rd.**

PT.-PT.	CUME	DIRECTION	STREET/LANDMARK
0.4	9.6	**R**	Onto unmarked **Clove Rd.** (first right turn you encounter)
2.0	11.6	**L**	**Valley Rd.** (after first climb in awhile)
0.2	11.8	**L**	**Mudtown Rd.** (T; no street sign)
2.9	14.7	**R**	**Rt. 23 North** (T)
0.2	14.9	**L**	**Brink Rd. Colesville Deli** on right after you make the turn. *If you are linking this route with* **Sunrise Mountain-High Point**, *turn around onto* **Rt. 23 South** *after stopping at the deli and pick up the* **Sunrise Mountain** *route at mile 19.9 of its cue sheet (page 104). Return to this cue sheet 32.5 miles later when you get back to the deli, and turn* **right** *onto* **Brink Rd.**
1.7	16.6	**L**	**Rt. 650 East/Deckertown Turnpike** (stop sign)
0.7	17.3	**S**	At stop sign, crossing Rt. 519
1.1	18.4	**R**	**Coykendall Rd.** Turn is shortly past church on right
1.5	19.9	**L**	**Rt. 519 South** (stop sign)
0.8	20.7	**R**	To continue on **Rt. 519 South** (T). Rt. 628 East goes left
0.1	20.8	**L**	**Holland Rd.**
1.9	22.7	**L**	**Rt. 637 South** (T)
0.7	23.4	**S**	Cross Rt. 635
1.3	24.7	**S**	Cross Rt. 565 at stop sign onto **Roy Rd.** *(Paved alternate: Turn* **left** *onto* **Rt. 565**, *following Rt. 565 right at traffic light in 2 miles. Rejoin cue sheet at mile 28.1, making a* **left** *to continue on Rt. 565)*

PT.-PT.	CUME	DIRECTION	STREET/LANDMARK
0.9	25.6	**L**	Onto unpaved road at T. Spree Rd. goes right
1.2	26.8	**L**	At unmarked intersection. You will be on **Lewisburg Rd.**, which is paved
1.3	28.1	**S**	At intersection, onto **Rt. 565 North**
1.4	29.5	**L**	**Rt. 23 North** (T)
0.3	29.8	**R**	Into **A&P Shopping Center**. End of route

UPPER DELAWARE WATER GAP—35.4 or 55.9 MILES

*See the **Lower Delaware Water Gap** route on page 141 for a challenging tour (88.7 miles) of the entire region.*

Terrain: Flatter than you'd ever believe in this mountainous region. The only serious climb on the short route occurs on the way to Peters Valley. The long route contains some rolling terrain. Otherwise the going is easy.
Traffic: Extremely light to nonexistent, except slightly busy in Port Jervis and near the Dingman's bridge.
Road Conditions: Very smooth on Route 521. Otherwise, fair to good. One three-mile section of well-packed dirt road on the long route.
Points of Interest: Cycling on the quietest roads in New Jersey; great views of river and hills; **swimming** in the Delaware River; **Dingman's Falls**; **Peters Valley Craft Village**.

The National Park Service can be credited for the cyclist's paradise on the New Jersey side of the Delaware Water Gap National Recreation Area. Most residents in the area were evacuated in the mid-1960s in preparation for the construction of the Tocks Island Dam and flooding of a large piece of land for a new reservoir. No dams or reservoirs were ever built. The result was mile after mile of beautiful woods and farm vistas on traffic-free roads.

There are plans to increase the number of organized beaches and boat launches on the New Jersey side of the river, but until this happens (probably no earlier than the mid-1990s), cyclists can enjoy the tranquility of truly being away from it all within the boundaries of the most densely populated state in the country.

The starting point for this route is a school only two miles from Route 206. The northbound ride is through pleasant farm country, interspersed with woods and ponds. Upon reaching Port Jervis, across the border in New York State, head back into

New Jersey on Route 521, a smooth, gently rolling road through more farmland.

After crossing Route 206 you will be cycling on The Old Mine Road, one of the oldest roads in the country and route of copper and iron from New Jersey mines to Revolutionary-era furnaces in New York State. Plaques along the road explain the history of a nearby buildings, many of which predate the Revolution. Chances are good you will see deer crossing the road—you might even spy a black bear ambling by.

Before coming to the Dingman's Ferry Bridge, you might wish to divert off the route to an excellent swimming area in a quiet eddy of the Delaware River. Then cross into Pennsylvania on the wood-floored bridge, one of the few privately owned toll bridges in the country. Your destination on the Pennsylvania side is Dingman's Falls. Lock your bikes by the information building and hike up to this impressive cataract. A good lunch spot is the very soft "floor of the forest" under the pine trees at the top of the falls.

Returning to New Jersey, climb the only steep hill of the short route, on the quiet, shady Old Mine Road. At the bottom of the subsequent downhill is Peters Valley Craft Village, a small collection of shops and workshops. Here you can decide to return directly to the starting point two miles away or take an additional 18-mile loop to the south.

Long-route cyclists will encounter a beautiful well-packed dirt road running right next to the river much of the way. Look for a spring to fill your water bottles. You will also pass large and productive cornfields and some boarded-up historic structures that may someday be restored.

Once pavement is reached, the terrain of the long route rolls a bit more noticeably than that of the short route. The return run goes next to Flat Brook, the only stream in New Jersey with a native trout population. You'll pass the Walpack Inn, an excellent place for a memorable meal after the ride.

Directions to Starting Point: Sandyston-Walpack School is on Rt. 560, about two miles west of Route 206. Take Exit 34B

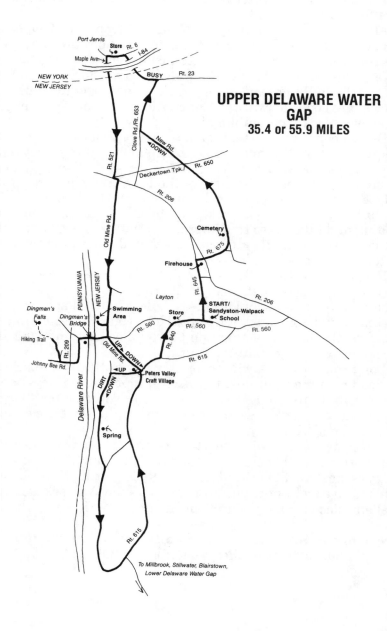

UPPER DELAWARE WATER GAP
35.4 or 55.9 MILES

off I-80 for Rt. 15 north. In 18 miles, where Rt. 15 ends, proceed straight onto Rt. 206 north. Look for the turn for Rt. 560 in 8 miles. The turn is also marked by a sign for Layton and Dingman's Toll Bridge.

PT.-PT.	CUME	DIRECTION	STREET/LANDMARK
0.0	0.0	**R**	Exit school and turn right onto **Rt. 560 West**
0.1	0.1	**R**	**Rt. 645 North** (toward Hainesville and Port Jervis)
2.8	2.9	**R**	**Rt. 675**. Turn just past the Sandyston Volunteer Fire Dept. Route sign is across Rt. 206
0.1	3.0	**S**	Cross Rt. 206 at stop sign onto road toward Abertown
0.3	3.3	**BL**	At unmarked fork. Street sign says DeGroat Rd., but it's unclear which road it refers to. You'll pass a cemetery on your left about 0.2 miles after turn
3.4	6.7	**S**	Cross Deckertown Tpk./Rt. 650. You are on **New Rd.**
2.1	8.8	**R**	**Clove Rd./Rt. 653** (T). *CAUTION: Turn is at the bottom of a hill and after a sharp curve—control speed*
3.9	12.7	**L**	**Rt. 23 North** (T). Ride on the shoulder. Watch for exiting and entering traffic at shopping center on right near bottom of hill
0.7	13.4	**BL**	**Rt. 6 West** (traffic light, just past I-84 overpass). Entering Port Jervis.
0.2	13.6		**Store** on right
0.1	13.7	**L**	**Maple Ave.** (second traffic light, before bridge). Captain John's Fish Market on corner

PT.-PT.	CUME	DIRECTION	STREET/LANDMARK
0.5	14.2		Go under I-84 and re-enter New Jersey on **Rt. 521 South**
7.0	21.2	**BL**	**Rt. 206 South** (T)
0.0	21.2	**R**	Immediate right onto narrow, unmarked **Old Mine Rd.** Pass a brown Delaware Water Gap sign immediately
3.3	24.5	**BR**	Unmarked fork. Cross small bridge immediately
3.1	27.6		Main route goes left at fork. If you wish to visit secluded **swimming area** on Delaware, turn right onto paved road. Proceed 0.6 miles. Road curves sharp right and becomes dirt. In an additional 0.1 mile, past the private house, turn into rocky, steep dirt driveway (opposite double hemlock tree) which leads to river. Return the way you came in, and bear right at the stop sign to resume the route on the **Old Mine Rd.**
0.3	27.9	**BR**	At stop sign toward Dingman's Bridge
0.2	28.1		Slowly cross wood-floored bridge, which is free for cyclists. Restrooms available at the canoe launch on left after crossing bridge. Welcome to Pennsylvania!
0.5	28.6	**L**	**"Road Not Maintained"**. Turn is first left past a double curve
0.3	28.9	**S**	Cross Rt. 209 at stop sign onto **Johnny Bee Rd.** There may not be a street sign here
0.4	29.3	**R**	Toward **Dingman's Falls** (rough road). Follow main road to end

PT.-PT.	CUME	DIRECTION	STREET/LANDMARK
0.7	30.0		End of road. Lock bike near information building and walk to falls. Afterwards, cycle back down the road you came in
0.7	30.7	**L**	**Johnny Bee Rd.** (T; no street sign)
0.5	30.2	**S**	Cross Rt. 209 at stop sign onto **"Road Not Maintained"**
0.2	30.4	**R**	At T toward Dingman's Bridge
0.5	30.9		Cross bridge back into New Jersey
0.2	31.1	**SR**	Unmarked **Old Mine Rd.** toward Peters Valley Craft Village
1.9	33.0		Stop sign at **Peters Valley** (*CAUTION: comes up at bottom of steep hill; control speed*)
			To return directly back to school (short route), turn **left** here onto **Rt. 615**. Resume cue sheet at Mile 54.2. The long route makes a **sharp right** onto an unmarked road. Keep Peters Valley store on your right
0.8	33.8	**L**	At unmarked T
0.7	34.5		Road becomes dirt at base of hill, so control speed. Mix of dirt and pavement follows
0.8	35.3		Road is definitely unpaved at this point
1.3	36.6		**Spring** on left
1.9	38.5	**R**	At T onto paved road
5.3	43.8		Turnoff for Millbrook, Stillwater and Blairstown (Rt. 615). *Cyclists doing the entire Delaware Water Gap and completing the Upper Gap route, turn* **right** *here and climb to Millbrook.* Upper Gap riders, go **straight** onto **Rt. 615 North**

PT.-PT.	CUME	DIRECTION	STREET/LANDMARK
9.7	53.5		**Peters Valley Store** on left. Curve right to continue on **Rt. 615 North**
0.7	54.2	**L**	*(Short Route Cume 33.7)* **Rt. 640** toward Layton and Dingman
1.3	55.5	**S**	*(Short Route Cume 35.0)* At blinking light onto **Rt. 560**. **Store** on left after intersection
0.4	55.9	**L**	*(Short Route Cume 35.4)* **Sandyston-Walpack School.** End of route

RIDES STARTING IN WARREN COUNTY

Warren County is Western New Jersey at its best. Rural, quiet, and mostly not yet suburbanized, cyclists can enjoy mile after mile of peace and tranquility as they pedal through this county.

The terrain varies from flat and easy in the well-named Tranquility Valley to hilly and hard closer to the Delaware River. Riding alongside the river is flat, and is one of the special treats of New Jersey cycling. This is because the river area is lightly developed and the roads along its shore are as sleepy as they were 100 years ago.

Allamuchy-Vienna-Johnsonburg features a new starting point away from the Allamuchy School (closed to cyclists on weekends). This short, pretty ride passes the sod farms of Great Meadows, climbs to Johnsonburg and Green Township and returns to the flatlands of the Tranquility Valley.

Belvidere-Hope-Stillwater cuts into Sussex County and covers a bit of the Delaware River on the Pennsylvania side, but mostly features the quiet roads of Warren. Blairstown is a pretty village halfway through the route that has ideal outdoor and indoor lunching spots. The intrepid might wish to take a glider flight at the nearby airport. River crossing is achieved on a pedestrian bridge. This ride is particularly nice in the fall.

Belvidere-Pohatcong covers the Delaware River south of Belvidere. A rider might feel as lazy as the river as he or she pedals slowly down the narrow, shaded roads, with cliffs on one side and river below. Return over farm roads passing 18th and 19th century stone houses and mills. Bring your camera!

Hackettstown-Bloomsbury is a long and somewhat challenging ride, but a delightful reward to the cyclist. As with much of Warren County, endless vistas of corn, cows, and green hills occupy the eye much of the time. The destination town of Bloomsbury has a good general store for lunch. On the way back you will pass an herb garden and a state-run pheasant farm.

Lower Delaware Water Gap is an up-and-back outing from the Visitor's Center on I-80 to Blue Mountain Lakes. The Delaware Water Gap National Recreation Area is extremely quiet on the New Jersey side, so you'll encounter little traffic. Be sure to visit Millbrook Village, a restored farmers' hamlet of the 19th Century.

ALLAMUCHY-VIENNA-JOHNSONBURG—25.9 MILES

The closing of Allamuchy School's parking lot to cyclist use necessitated some changes in cycling patterns in Tranquility Valley - Great Meadows area. The result of some map pondering is this beautiful new RIDE GUIDE *route, starting from the nearby Panther Valley shopping center.*

Terrain: Mostly rolling hills. Nothing too horribly steep except, unfortunately, the climb up from the former finishing point at Allamuchy School to the current finishing point at Panther Valley shopping center.

Traffic: Very light, except moderate on the short stretch of Rt. 46 and on Rt. 517 at the end.

Road Conditions: Good to excellent. A little choppy on Rt. 517 near the end, but all the quiet back roads are smoothly paved.

Points of Interest: Great Meadows sod fields — some of the green grass in the distance will soon be in America's great baseball stadiums; the quaint and somewhat dilapidated hamlet of **Johnsonburg**; fine farm country of the **Tranquility Valley.**

Allamuchy and **Tranquility Valley** have been among the most popular cycling destinations in northern New Jersey for many years, because of the unspoiled beauty of the gently rolling farm country and the proximity to I-80 of the most popular starting point, the Allamuchy School. Unfortunately the school became a bit too popular and the township school board decided to close the parking lot on weekends, partly because of the actions of a few cyclists who used nearby fields as bathrooms.

RIDE GUIDE has moved the starting point for one route in the area to the Andover (see **Andover-Swartswood Lake**, page 90), and the start for this route is the Panther Valley shopping center, just one mile south of the school. The publishers ask readers to respect the need of the retailers in the shopping center to retain parking places for their customers and park as far away from the stores as possible, so as not to wear out your welcome. There is a fine restaurant/ice cream parlor in the shopping center to patronize after the ride and by doing so you will help the storekeepers see that it is a good thing to have cyclists use their parking lot.

The shopping center is higher in elevation than Allamuchy School, which means a great downhill at the beginning of the route and a bit of a climb near the end. In between, most of the terrain is gently rolling, with quite a bit of near-flat cycling.

Begin by zooming down Cat Swamp Road and riding into the small settlement of Vienna alongside some pretty farms.

A short ride along a still-countrylike Rt. 46 brings you by a food store in Great Meadows, then it's off to Shades of Death Road.

This street with the scary name goes by the huge sod farms of Great Meadows, farmed by several generations of the same families that came to the U.S. from Poland and Eastern Europe. Some of the sod growing in the flat valley off to the right will be transplanted to famous stadiums and golf courses across the country.

Shades of Death Rd enters the woods after awhile and passes Ghost Lake, which is a good place to stop and dip your toes into the water (swimming is not permitted). Back on the bike, skirt the western end of the flat Tranquility Valley and take a rolling ride alongside of some attractive horse farms on Bear Creek Rd. Pedal back in time by cycling down the main street of Johnsonburg, a hamlet that defines "quiet". There is a small store for refreshments.

The ride into Sussex County's Green Township is a bit of a climb. Another small store is available here, before the route heads east and back toward Allamuchy.

Pass the school which used to be a hotbed of weekend cycling activity (and still is in May for the annual MS-150 fundraiser ride for the Northern New Jersey Chapter of the National Multiple Sclerosis Society). Still another small store

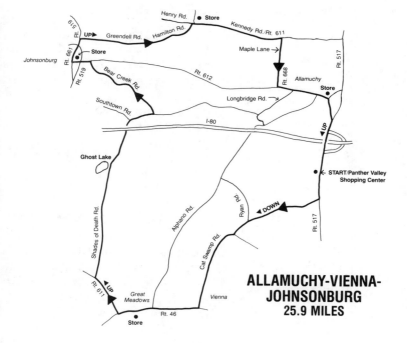

ALLAMUCHY-VIENNA-
JOHNSONBURG
25.9 MILES

can provide the rider with a cooling drink of juice before the big climb back toward Panther Valley.

Directions to Starting Point: The route begins in the **Panther Valley Shopping Center**, about 1 mile south of I-80 Exit 19 off Rt. 517. Please park away from the retail stores. A good place to eat and relax after the ride is BLD's Restaurant in the shopping center, a Morris Area Freewheeler post-ride hangout for several decades.

PT.-PT.	CUME	DIRECTION	STREET/LANDMARK
0.0	0.0	R	**Rt. 517 South**
0.7	0.7	R	After brief climb, onto **Cat Swamp Rd.** Enjoy tremendous downhill, and watch speed on curves!
2.0	2.7	S	At yield sign onto **Ryan Rd.** Ryan Rd. also goes off to the right at this intersection
0.4	3.1	R	At T onto unmarked road
2.0	5.1	R	**Rt. 46** in Vienna (T)
1.2	6.3		**Nykun's Store** on left in Great Meadows
0.2	6.5	R	**Rt. 611**, toward Mountain Lake and Hope
1.6	8.1	R	**Shades of Death Rd.** Turn is at top of hill, with no street sign. There is a sign pointing for Grabowski's Greenhouses
3.7	11.8		**Ghost Lake** on left
0.5	12.3		Curve right after I-80 underpass to continue on **Shades of Death Rd.** Southtown Rd. goes left

PT.-PT.	CUME	DIRECTION	STREET/LANDMARK
0.7	13.0	**L**	**Bear Creek Rd.** Street sign is on the back of the stop sign on the intersecting road; turn is before a little creek bridge
2.6	15.6	**L**	**Rt. 612** (T; no sign)
0.1	15.7	**S**	At stop sign, crossing Rt. 519
0.2	15.9	**R**	**Rt. 661** (T; no sign). Main street of **Johnsonburg**; **store** on right in 0.1 miles
0.3	16.2	**S**	At stop sign onto **Rt. 519 North**
0.2	16.4	**R**	**Greendell Rd.** Turn is opposite cemetery. Climb short, steep hill after turn. Road changes name upon entry into Sussex County to **Hamilton Rd.**
3.2	19.6	R	**Henry Rd.** (T). Road changes name at Junction Rt. 611 (0.1 miles after turn) to **Kennedy Rd./Rt. 611.** For a **store,** turn left at Rt. 611; store is on right in about 100 feet
2.0	21.6	R	**Maple Lane.** Becomes **Rt. 668**
1.5	23.1	L	**Rt. 612 South** (T)
1.4	24.5	R	At unmarked T in Allamuchy hamlet. **Store** on left before turn. Commence tough climb
0.3	24.8	BR	**Rt. 517 South**, at stop sign. Continue climbing, crossing over I-80. Check out view of Delaware Water Gap on your right!
1.1	25.9	R	**Panther Valley Shopping Center**. End of route

BELVIDERE-HOPE-STILLWATER—52.8 MILES

This route is based on the course devised by Max Gerlach, a Morris Area Freewheeler who is well known as a person who loves a good view attained without excessive effort.

Terrain: Gently rolling, for the most part. A couple of short climbs and short, fast descents.
Traffic: Light, except on the few numbered highways. Busy around the Columbia intersection of Rts. 94 and 80
Road Conditions: Very well paved, with a few rough roads. No dirt.
Points of Interest: Hope and **Stillwater** (picturesque hamlets with interesting old buildings); **Blairstown** (village with old Main Street, and a park with pond); **Blairstown Airport** (glider rides available); **footbridge over Delaware River**; riding along the river and through beautiful farm country.

The quiet back roads of three counties are explored on this route. Starting in Warren County, this ride goes into Sussex, back into Warren then over to Northampton County, Pennsylvania.

Cyclists will encounter very few major climbs over this 52-miler, so energetic novices might use this ride to increase their maximum distance.

Start by heading to the Moravian settlement of Hope. Some interesting stone buildings line the main road, and a luncheonette is available for snacks.

Next head north into Johnsonburg. A popular activity in this very small community is driving up and down the main street with one's dog hanging out the window. Fortunately, none of them seem to bite.

Some pretty views are visible after a short climb near Stillwater—the hills all the way to the Delaware Water Gap and beyond are visible on a clear day. Stillwater has a pretty inn on a stream, an old mill and a general store.

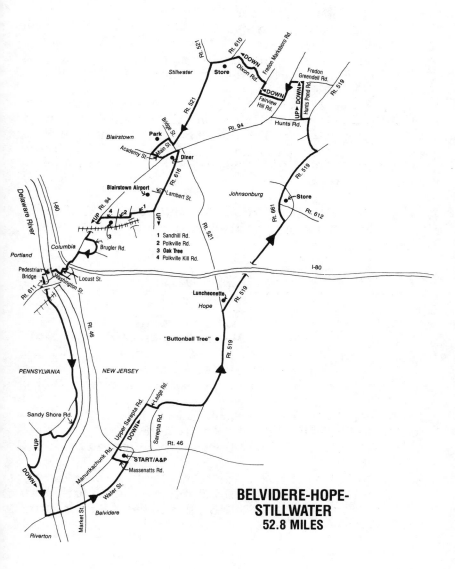

1 Sandhill Rd.
2 Polkville Rd.
3 Oak Tree
4 Polkville Kill Rd.

**BELVIDERE-HOPE-
STILLWATER
52.8 MILES**

Near the halfway point, the village of Blairstown has a park with a pond where you can picnic. If it is cool or wet, a cozy diner is available on Rt. 94. Look for the unusual stone arch over the sidewalk by the library.

You might wish to take a short side trip to the Blairstown Airport. Glider rides are available here, and even if you don't go up, the quiet soaring craft are fun to watch. It's a homey airport with a nice little restaurant where you can walk right out onto the field if you wish.

Soon you will cross into Pennsylvania on a pedestrians-only bridge, one of two over the Delaware (the other is near Washington's Crossing). The ride along the river is on a quiet road with small summer homes. Near Belvidere you'll encounter a hill, but soon after that you cross the river and return to the starting point.

Directions to Starting Point: The **Belvidere A&P** is on the left side of Rt. 46 heading west, approximately 20 miles west of I-80 Exit 26.

PT.-PT.	CUME	DIRECTION	STREET/LANDMARK
0.0	0.0	R	Exit rear of A&P onto **Massenatts Rd.** and turn right
0.1	0.1	R	**Manunkachunk Rd.** (stop sign).
0.1	0.2	S	Cross Rt. 46 at stop sign onto **Upper Sarepta Rd.**
1.1	1.3	R	**Ledge Rd.** Turn is at the bottom of a hill and easy to miss!
0.2	1.5	L	**Sarepta Rd.** (T)
1.0	2.5	L	**Rt. 519 North** (T)
3.9	6.4		**"George Washington Buttonball Tree"** on left
1.3	7.7	R	At blinking light in center of Hope to continue on **Rt. 519 North. Luncheonette** on left just after turn

PT.-PT.	CUME	DIRECTION	STREET/LANDMARK
5.3	13.0	L	**Rt. 661** (Rt. 519 widens at this corner)
1.3	14.3		**Store** on right, in Johnsonburg
0.1	14.4	S	At stop sign onto **Rt. 519 North**
2.2	16.6	L	To continue on **Rt. 519 North**. Road is also called **Wintermute Rd.**
1.2	17.8	L	**Hunts Rd.** (may not be a street sign). Road goes uphill into a wooded glen with a small brook. You'll pass an old gristmill on the left
0.1	17.9	R	Unmarked road (first right turn), which goes steeply uphill
1.5	19.4	L	At T at bottom of hill
0.6	20.0	L	**Rt. 94 South** (T)
1.0	21.0	R	**Fairview Hill Rd.** *CAUTION: Control your speed on the extremely steep descent!*
0.8	21.8	R	**Fredon Marksboro Rd.** (T)
0.3	22.1	L	**Dixon Rd.** Turn at red barn. Note waterwheel behind this building. *Watch speed as you continue to descend*
1.4	23.5	L	**Rt. 610** (T). Cross bridge into Stillwater
0.2	23.7		**Store** on left
0.1	23.8	L	**Rt. 521 South**
5.5	29.3	R	**Bridge St.** in Blairstown
0.1	29.4	L	**Main St., Blairstown** (second left turn)
0.1	29.5		**Park** on right (by dam) just before library archway. Then continue down **Main Street**
0.2	29.7	L	**Academy St.**
0.0	29.7	L	Immediate left onto **Rt. 94 North** (T)

PT.-PT.	CUME	DIRECTION	STREET/LANDMARK
0.1	29.8		**Diner** on right
0.3	30.1	R	**Rt. 616**, toward Cedar Lake/Lake Susquehanna
2.4	32.5		Turn **right** at **Lambert Rd.** for sidetrip to **Blairstown Airport** (glider rides; restaurant; plane watching)
0.4	32.9	R	**Sand Hill Rd.**
1.2	34.1	L	At T
0.1	34.2	R	Immediate right onto **Polkville Rd.** (no sign). Do not go under tunnel
1.1	35.3	S	Onto **Polkville Kill Rd.** (no sign). Keep large oak tree on your left
1.8	37.1	L	**Rt. 94 South** (T)
1.1	38.2	L	**Brugler Rd.**
0.6	38.8	R	At T after old stone bridge onto unmarked road. Cross steel bridge
0.6	39.4	L	**Rt. 94 South**
0.4	39.8		Follow **Rt. 94**. Do not exit for I-80 or Rt. 46. *Watch for trucks entering and exiting!*
0.4	40.2	R	At exit for **Columbia**. Curve around to the right at end of ramp
0.1	40.3	L	**Locust St.** (stop sign)
0.1	40.4	R	**Washington St.** (T)
0.1	40.5	L	Cross **pedestrian bridge** over river into Pennsylvania
0.1	40.6	L	**Rt. 611** through Portland, Pa. Continue **straight** after underpass for car bridge and cross railroad tracks. Follow road along Delaware River.
5.5	46.1	L	**Sandy Shore Rd.**
1.2	47.3	L	At T
1.1	48.4	L	Curve left (toward Riverton)

PT.-PT.	CUME	DIRECTION	STREET/LANDMARK
1.2	49.6	**SL**	At stop sign on downhill switchback (*CAUTION—watch speed*) toward Riverton and Belvidere
1.1	50.7	**L**	At T (Riverton Restaurant on corner) over bridge back into New Jersey
0.4	51.1	**S**	At traffic light
1.6	52.7	**L**	At sign pointing toward Rt. 46 (unmarked **Massenatts Rd.**)
0.1	52.8	**R**	Into rear of **A&P** parking lot. End of route

BELVIDERE-POHATCONG—44.3 MILES

In the interest of covering every scenic mile in New Jersey along the Delaware River, RIDE GUIDE *presents this route. It explores the Warren County hills without being hilly!*

Terrain: Gently rolling, with a few short, steep pitches on River Rd.

Traffic: On most of the route, you could fall asleep in the middle of the road and not worry about getting run over (i.e., you'll see more cows than cars). It is somewhat busier in Phillipsburg and Belvidere and on Rt. 519 on the way back.

Road Conditions: Excellent. Sleepy roads don't take a beating, so they stay fairly smooth.

Points of Interest: One of the quietest corners of New Jersey, with lots of views of the Delaware River and various tributaries; many stone houses dating to the 1700's; **Warren County Farmer's Fair** (mid-August).

If one part of northern New Jersey can be called "undiscovered" (by the auto tourist and, until recently, even by many bicyclists), it's this corner of Warren County. Pretty, narrow, untrafficked roads parallel the Delaware River and some of its tributary streams, including Pohatcong Creek. The high roads give commanding views of the Delaware Water Gap, cornfields, and cows.

Start by cycling south out of Belvidere, the county seat town that seems just like another country crossroads. Immediately you'll ride by the Delaware River. Those huge cooling towers on the Pennsylvania side belong to a conventional (non-nuclear) power plant.

The road occasionally goes inland past large cornfields, then returns to the river. You'll experience an occasional short, steep climb but the road is mostly flat. Much of the time a large cliff is on your left, a railroad track is on your right and the river is

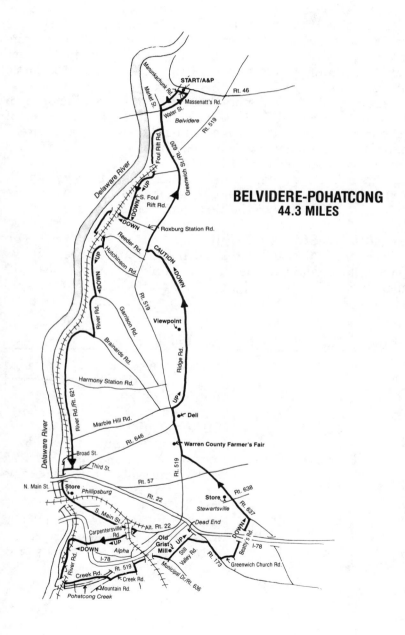

Manunkachunk Rd.
START/A&P
Rt. 46
Market St.
Massenatt's Rd.
Water St.
Belvidere
Rt. 519
Foul Rift Rd.
Greenwich St./Rt. 620
DOWN
UP
S. Foul Rift Rd.
DOWN

BELVIDERE-POHATCONG
44.3 MILES

Roxburg Station Rd.
Reeder Rd.
Hutchinson Rd.
CAUTION
DOWN
Rt. 519
River Rd.
Garrison Rd.
UP
DOWN
Brainards Rd.
Viewpoint
Harmony Station Rd.
Ridge Rd.
River Rd./Rt. 621
Marble Hill Rd.
UP
Rt. 646
Deli
Broad St.
Warren County Farmer's Fair
Delaware River
Third St.
Rt. 57
N. Main St.
Store
Phillipsburg
Rt. 519
Rt. 22
Store
Rt. 638
Stewartsville
Rt. 637
S. Main St.
Alt. Rt. 22
Dead End
DOWN
Carpentersville Rd.
UP
Old Grist Mill
Beatty's Rd.
I-78
Alpha
DOWN
Still Valley Rd.
Rt. 173
Greenwich Church Rd.
I-78
River Rd.
Rt. 519
Creek Rd.
Municipal Dr./Rt. 636
Creek Rd.
Mountain Rd.
Pohatcong Creek
Delaware River

down below the railroad. Look for wild raspberries growing in sweet profusion in late July and early August.

After going through the old river town of Phillipsburg, ride south into more quiet river country. Turn back along the Pohatcong Creek, where you might find a shady spot to eat lunch. Swimming in the creek isn't recommended due to cattle farms upstream.

Pass a number of old stone houses in this area, including a mill dating to the 1700s. Ride carefully through a number of long, dark tunnels under railroad embankments. A food store is available in Stewartsville. Next, head into Harmony Township on moderately travelled Rt. 519.

Ridge Rd. is a special treat. The climb to get here is short, the views on top are incredible. In warm weather hawks circle overhead on their way to the Delaware Water Gap.

Directions to Starting Point: The **A&P in Belvidere** is on Rt. 46. From I-80, use Exit 12. Turn left (south) toward Hope. In Hope, keep going straight at the blinker light onto Rt. 519 South. In 7 miles, turn right at the traffic light onto Rt. 46 West. The A&P will be on your left in about a mile.

PT.-PT.	CUME	DIRECTION	STREET/LANDMARK
0.0	0.0	**R**	Exit the **rear** of the A&P parking lot and turn **right** onto unmarked **Massenatt's Rd.**
0.1	0.1	**L**	**Manunkachunk Rd.** (stop sign)
1.4	1.5	**L**	**Market St.** (T)
0.3	1.8	**S**	At the traffic light in Belvidere, crossing Water St. onto Rt. **622 South**. This will eventually become **Greenwich St.**
0.7	2.5	**R**	**Foul Rift Rd.**
1.9	4.4	**R**	**South Foul Rift Rd.** Turn is just past one-lane railroad underpass
1.5	5.9	**R**	At T and stop sign (no street sign).

PT.-PT.	CUME	DIRECTION	STREET/LANDMARK
			Head downhill, under railroad underpass
1.4	7.3	**BR**	At fork after railroad underpass. Reeder Rd. goes left
0.1	7.4	**R**	**River Rd.**
1.4	8.8	**R**	**Garrison Rd.** (T)
0.6	9.4	**R**	**Brainards Rd.** (T)
0.3	9.7	**L**	**River Rd./Rt. 621 South**. Ignore any "road closed" signs. Bikes can get through
6.4	16.1	**R**	At stop sign and T in Phillipsburg (Ice cream store in front of you)
0.1	16.2	**R**	**Third St.** Do not go onto Easton Bridge
0.0	16.2	**L**	**Broad St.** (stop sign)
0.5	16.7	**S**	At traffic light. You are now on **North Main St.**
0.2	16.9		**Deli** on left. You are now on **South Main St.**
0.1	17.0		Cross bridge over railroad
0.2	17.2	**BR**	To continue on **South Main St./ Alt. Rt. 22 East**
1.6	18.8	**SR**	**Carpentersville Rd.** (no street sign). Turn is just past double railroad underpass, the second of which is a huge stone arch bridge. Road goes uphill and back under both railroad underpasses
0.8	19.6	**R**	Toward Carpentersville (do not go toward Alpha). Road crosses bridge over I-78
1.7	21.3	**L**	Curve left onto **River Rd.**
2.2	23.5	**BL**	At fork after railroad underpass, onto unmarked **Creek Rd.** Do not cross green bridge over Pohatcong

PT.-PT.	CUME	DIRECTION	STREET/LANDMARK
			Creek (there is a good lunch spot on the other side, however)
1.2	24.7	**L**	At T after crossing creek, to continue on **Creek Rd.** Mountain Rd. goes right
1.2	25.9	**L**	**Rt. 519 North** (T; no street sign)
0.3	26.2	**R**	**Municipal Dr./Rt. 636 East**
0.5	26.7		*CAUTION: Long, dark tunnel under railroad embankment*
0.3	27.0	**L**	**Still Valley Rd.** Note old grist mill on left after turn
0.9	27.9	**R**	At point where road straight ahead dead ends into I-78 embankment
0.2	28.1	**R**	**Rt. 173 East** (T; no street sign; interchange with I-78 is visible to the left)
0.4	28.5	**L**	**Greenwich Church Rd.** (toward Old Greenwich Presbyterian Church)
0.1	28.6	**L**	At unmarked fork with tree in island. You will be on **Beatty's Rd.**
0.7	29.3		Go under I-78
0.3	29.6	**L**	At T onto unmarked **Rt. 637**
1.4	31.0	**S**	Cross Rt. 638 at blinking light in center of Stewartsville. **Store** on left after intersection
0.9	31.9	**S**	Cross Rt. 57 at stop sign. Continue on **Rt. 637 North** toward Harmony
1.0	32.9	**R**	**Rt. 519 North** (T)
1.0	33.9		Site of **Warren County Farmer's Fair** on left (mid-August)
0.7	34.6	**R**	At T to continue on **Rt. 519 North** (Rt. 646 goes left). **Deli** on right after turn
0.5	35.1	**R**	**Ridge Rd.** (at top of hill)

PT.-PT.	CUME	DIRECTION	STREET/LANDMARK
1.2	36.3		Great **view** of Delaware Water Gap on left
3.2	39.5	**R**	**Rt. 519 North** (T). *CAUTION: Control speed as you head downhill to this stop sign. Road becomes very steep and curvy at the end*
1.6	41.1	**S**	**Rt. 620 North**. Rt. 519 goes right
1.6	42.7	**R**	At traffic light in the center of Belvidere onto **Water St./Rt. 620 North**
1.6	44.3	**L**	**Massenatt's Rd.** toward Rt. 46 West
0.0	44.3	**R**	Immediate **right** into rear of **A&P Shopping Center**. End of route

HACKETTSTOWN-BLOOMSBURY—51.9 MILES

This classic route appeared in the first edition of RIDE GUIDE, *and continues to be an appealing, challenging route.*

Terrain: Hilly on the first half, including a few long climbs and delightfully extended descents. Rolling to hilly on the return half.
Traffic: Very light, except moderate near Hackettstown, Bloomsbury and on Rt. 519.
Road Conditions: Fair to good, with some patchy pavement.
Points of Interest: Pequest Trout Hatchery; quaint small towns of **Stewartsville, Bloomsbury** and **Port Murray**; **Warren County Farmer's Fair** (mid-August); **Well Sweep Herb Farm**; **Rockport Pheasant Farm.**

This beautiful rural ride rewards the cyclist with quiet roads, tremendous views and a sense of exhilaration and accomplishment, owing to some hilly terrain. The four-mile descent into Harmony makes it all worthwhile.

Leaving Hackettstown, ride over a mountain (a long hill, anyway) into the Pequest Valley. The trout hatchery is worth a visit if you are a fishing enthusiast.

Next, spin your way south over hill and dale, passing cornfields and woods. Maps call the big climb on Rt. 647 "Montana." Pretty soon you'll see the cyclist's favorite yellow diamond sign: a truck pointing down a precipitous incline: hill ahead!

In the midst of the Harmony downhill, rest your brake hands at the fruit stand and enjoy some peaches or cider, depending on the time of year. Past Harmony, it continues downhill (a little gentler) all the way into Bloomsbury. En route are the grounds of the Warren County Farmers' Fair, a genuine agricultural event that takes place in the middle of August.

The general store in Bloomsbury has a picnic table on the lawn for lunch, or you can eat by the nearby bridge over the Musconetcong River. The return route is less steep but still roll-

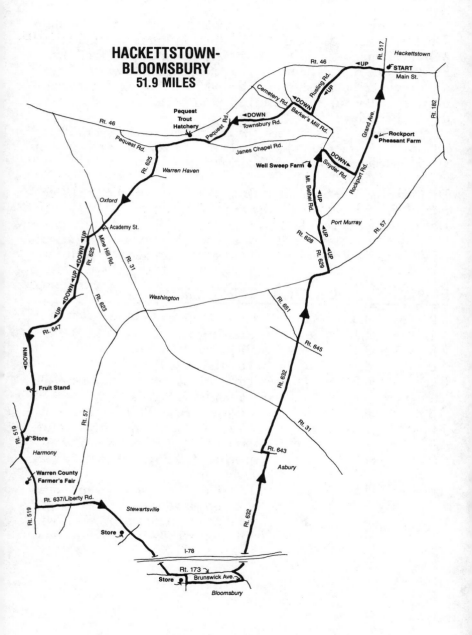

HACKETTSTOWN-BLOOMSBURY
51.9 MILES

ing, with views long and far of corn-covered hillsides around Asbury.

Heading into Port Murray is another climb, but worthwhile. The town itself has some old buildings dating from its days as a Morris Canal port, and an interesting antique store. Well Sweep Farm, at the top of the hill, has a colorful garden where flowers are grown to be dried, and a formal herb garden. The farm is open Tuesday through Saturday, and is closed Sunday, Monday and holidays.

The final point of interest is the state-run Rockport Pheasant Farm. Numerous pheasants are on display, and occasionally a peacock struts around the grounds.

Directions to Starting Point: The route begins at the corner of **Main St. (Rt. 46) and High St. (Rt. 517)** in Hackettstown. From I-80 Exit 19, proceed 5 miles south on Rt. 517 into Hackettstown. There are two municipal parking lots on either side of Rt. 517 just before the intersection of Rt. 46.

PT.-PT.	CUME	DIRECTION	STREET/LANDMARK
0.0	0.0	R	**Main St./Rt. 46 West**
1.1	1.1	BL	**Rusling Rd.** toward Mt. Bethel
2.0	3.1	R	**Barkers Mill Rd.** (T)
1.0	4.1	L	**Townsbury Rd.**
0.1	4.2	L	To continue on **Townsbury Rd.** Cemetery Rd. goes right
2.3	6.5	L	**Pequest Rd.** (T; no sign)
1.0	7.5	R	At T, to continue on **Pequest Rd.** Janes Chapel Rd. goes left
0.2	7.7		**Pequest Trout Hatchery** on right
0.5	8.2	L	**Rt. 625** (toward Warren Acres/ Warren Haven)
0.5	8.7	R	At Warren Haven entrance to continue on **Rt. 625**

PT.-PT.	CUME	DIRECTION	STREET/LANDMARK
2.8	11.5	S	Cross Rt. 31 at stop sign to continue on **Rt. 625/Academy St.**
0.4	11.9	S	Cross Mine Hill Rd. at stop sign
0.1	12.0	L	At T to continue on **Rt. 625**
2.0	14.0	S	Cross Rt. 623 at stop sign
1.2	15.2	BR	At stop sign (*CAUTION: at bottom of steep hill; control speed!*) onto **Rt. 647**
2.5	17.7		Begin huge downhill
2.8	20.5		**Fruit stand** on right
1.7	22.2	L	**Rt. 519** (T)
0.1	22.3		**Store** on left
0.1	22.4	L	To continue on **Rt. 519**
0.7	23.1		**Warren County Farmers Fair** on right (mid-August)
1.0	24.1	L	**Rt. 637/Liberty Rd.**
1.0	25.1	S	Cross Rt. 57 at stop sign
1.0	26.1	S	At blinker light in Stewartsville; **store** on right before intersection
1.7	27.8		Road goes under I-78
1.1	28.9	L	**Rt. 173 East** (stop sign)
0.6	29.5	R	Toward **Bloomsbury**. Cross Musconetcong River immediately.
0.1	29.6	L	Unmarked **Brunswick Ave.** Good lunch spot and **store** on right before making turn
0.5	30.1	L	**Wilson St.**
0.1	30.2	L	**Rt. 173 West** (T; no sign)
0.1	30.3	SR	**Rt. 632** toward Asbury (no street sign). Go under I-78 shortly after turn
4.7	35.0	L	**Rt. 643** (T)
0.1	35.1	R	**Rt. 632 East**
2.7	37.8	S	Cross Rt. 31 at stop sign

PT.-PT.	CUME	DIRECTION	STREET/LANDMARK
2.0	39.8	S	Crossing Rts. 645 and 651. Continue on **Rt. 632 East**
2.4	42.2	BR	**Rt. 57 North** (T)
0.3	42.5	L	At blinking light onto **Rt. 629**, toward Port Murray and Rockport
1.6	44.1	BR	To continue on **Rt. 629** toward Hackettstown and Rockport; Rt. 628 goes left
0.7	44.8	BL	**Mt. Bethel Rd.** (Rockport Rd. goes right)
1.0	45.8		**Well Sweep Herb Farm** on left
0.7	46.5	R	**Snyder Rd.** No street sign! Turn is just past an old stone church with an old graveyard (on right). *CAUTION: Control your speed on Snyder Rd.'s curvy downhill section*
1.2	47.7	L	**Rockport Rd.** (T; no street sign)
1.1	48.8		**Rockport Pheasant Farm** on right
1.7	50.5		*CAUTION: Single-lane underpass.* You are now entering Hackettstown on **Grand Ave.**
1.4	51.9		Cross Main St. onto **High St.** End of route

LOWER DELAWARE WATER GAP—30.2 MILES

The original Delaware Water Gap ride published in the first edition of RIDE GUIDE *travelled from I-80 to Dingman's Falls. Now this route is shorter, good for a leisurely day of cycling and relaxing by the river or ponds and streams along the way. Dingman's Falls, Peters Valley and Port Jervis are covered by the Upper Delaware Water Gap route. Directions are given here for ambitious cyclists who wish to do the entire Delaware Water Gap, a tour of 88.7 miles (less if various shortcuts shown on the maps are taken).*

Terrain: Rolling, with a major climb from Millbrook to Blue Mountain Lake.
Traffic: Extremely light.
Road Conditions: Fair to good.
Points of Interest: Numerous streamside and pondside picnic areas; **Millbrook Historic Village**; **Delaware River.**

The **Delaware Water Gap** is quiet and serene as National Recreation Areas go. The main road you will cycle on is generally only used by fishermen, hunters and the occasional sightseer. Thus you will go mile after mile through beautiful woodlands and see very few cars. This may change in the mid-1990s if a plan to "develop" the area with more beaches and boat-launching ramps becomes a reality, but for now most Gap visitors stick to the Pennsylvania side, leaving the New Jersey side with excellent quiet cycling.

You'll be riding up and back on the Old Mine Road, one of the oldest continuously used thoroughfares in the country. This now-sleepy area resounded with miners and transport wagons in the 17th and 18th Century as copper and iron made their way from the earth to the forges further north.

Millbrook Village shows what a typical farming village was like in the 18th and 19th Centuries. Demonstrations of various aspects of farm village life are given. The restored buildings and ponds are very photogenic on a sunny fall day, so be sure to bring a camera.

The turn-around point, up a long climb, is Blue Mountain Lakes, a serene setting for lunch or a quick cooling dip. The lower lake is a seven-minute hike from the parking lot (bikes are not allowed on the trails). Be sure to take the trail to the right as you enter the trail system. After returning to your bike, the whiz downhill from the lake has a glorious view well into Pennsylvania that will make you forget the strain of the climb.

Directions to Starting Point: The **Delaware Water Gap Visitor's Center** is right off I-80. Take the last exit before the bridge to Pennsylvania, turn left to go under the highway, and the visitor's center will be on your right.

PT.-PT.	CUME	DIRECTION	STREET/LANDMARK
0.0	0.0	**L**	Out of Visitor's Center parking lot onto road paralleling I-80. Continue under highway
0.5	0.5		"3 Minute Traffic Light." You will have 3 minutes to ride 0.3 miles on a one-lane road when the light turns green before oncoming traffic is released
2.8	3.3		Entrance to **Worthington State Forest** camping area on left
4.8	8.1		**Poxono Boat Launch** area (restroom) on left
1.9	10.0		**Van Campen Glen** picnic area on right
1.8	11.8		**Watergate Recreation Area** (pond) on right
0.5	12.3	**L**	At fork, toward Walpack. **Millbrook Village** restoration on right just past fork

PT.-PT.	CUME	DIRECTION	STREET/LANDMARK
1.6	13.9	R	At sign for **Blue Mountain Lakes.** *Riders doing the entire Delaware Water Gap should skip the climb to Blue Mountain Lakes and go* **straight** *here for 0.7 additional downhill miles to the Flat Brook Bridge.* CAUTION: Watch your speed on the hill! *At the stop sign, turn* **right** *and join the* **Upper Delaware Water Gap** *route at Mile 43.8, page 115. Ride that route to its start/end point, then loop back from the beginning, turning right at Mile 43.8 and climbing up the hill. In 2.3 miles you'll reach Millbrook, where you'll resume the* **Lower Delaware Water Gap** *route cue sheet at Mile 17.9*
1.2	15.1	L	Into parking lot for **Blue Mountain Lakes**. Lock bikes and walk up to lake (bikes not allowed on trails). After visiting the lake, turn **right** out of the parking lot to cycle back down the road you came up
1.2	16.3	L	At T at bottom of steep hill. Watch speed!
1.6	17.9	R	At fork. **Millbrook Village** on left
0.5	18.4		**Watergate Recreation Area** on left
1.8	20.2		**Van Campen Glen** picnic area on left
1.9	22.1		**Poxono Boat Launch** area (restroom) on right

4.8	26.9		Entrance to **Worthington State Forest** camping area on right
2.8	29.7		"3 Minute Traffic Light"
0.5	30.2	**R**	Into **Delaware Water Gap Visitor's Center**. End of route

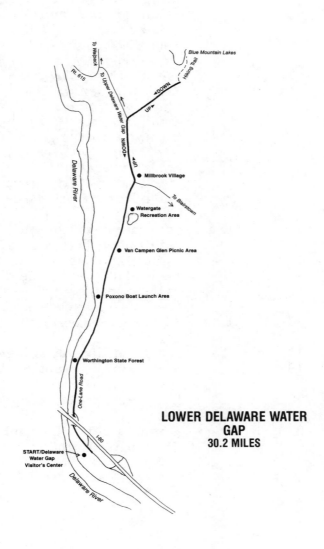

Blue Mountain Lakes

To Walpack

Rt. 615

To Upper Delaware Water Gap

DOWN

UP

Hiking Trail

DOWN

UP

Millbrook Village

To Blairstown

Delaware River

Watergate Recreation Area

Van Campen Glen Picnic Area

Poxono Boat Launch Area

Worthington State Forest

One-Lane Road

I-90

START/Delaware Water Gap Visitor's Center

Delaware River

LOWER DELAWARE WATER GAP
30.2 MILES

OFF-ROAD RIDES

Section by Ellen R. Otto

Welcome to off-road bicycling. This is also known as mountain biking. This section contains five different rides. Most are suitable for either cross or hybrid bikes, with the exception of parts of Ramapo State Forest and parts of South Mountain Reservation.

Two of the rides are old railroad lines which are now multi-use paths (used for runners, hikers and horseback riders). Please be careful and yield to other people using the trails or we, the mountain bikers, will be denied access.

The first trail is the **Little Falls Railroad Ride**, and is easy. This trail is 8.4 miles round trip and is quick and fun.

Patriots' Path in Morristown has some areas which go through the woods, then open into meadows full of wildflowers. This path is crossed by many deer, due in part to large tracts of undeveloped lands. To ride both routes described, allow four hours.

Ramapo State Forest features a glorious decent, a bit of a climb, a beautiful lake and ruins of an old mansion with fine views of New York to the east, Wanaque Reservoir to the west and a good part of North Jersey to the south.

South Mountain Reservation trails are for strong intermediate to advanced riders. Front suspension is strongly recommended. There are so many turnoffs on this trail that a map is highly recommended.

Sussex Branch is an old railroad bed that goes through a tunnel, by many lakes and pretty woods.

Before You Bike Off-Road: There are certain things which are a must when mountain biking. Never, ever leave home without a good quality Snell or ANSI helmet. These types of helmets absorbs the impact of any fall so your head doesn't. Also, never ride alone!

Always use the buddy system. Tools should be brought along on any ride, and the basics of any tool kit should include: a tire patch kit and tire irons, pump and spare inner-tube to fit your rims, Allen wrenches or keys and a Crescent wrench. For rides further away from your home or car, besides what is listed above it is helpful to carry a chain tool with extra links and pins for putting back the chain. Of course, riders should have some knowledge of bike repairs, which can be obtained either from books or good bike shops which usually offer maintenance clinics.

Please check your bike the night before a long ride. This check should take five to fifteen minutes to ensure a perfect ride. Check the brakes to be sure they are hitting the rims correctly and are working well. Check the tire pressure, the walls of the tires to make sure there are no cracks, tears or threads showing through the side wall. Adjust seat height, and make sure all bolts and cranks are tight. Check that the gears shift smoothly and don't jump around, and that the chain is lubricated well and no links are stiff. Once all this is checked, you can go out and ride without worrying about your bike.

Carry two large water bottles in each ride, tissues, some kind of energy snack, a basic first aid kit and a tool kit, as described above. But with all that said and done, get ready to enjoy the beautiful sights and pleasures of mountain biking. Enjoy!

LITTLE FALLS RAILROAD RIDE—7.2 MILES

Terrain: Flat to gentle grade changes, except for a hill to reach the rail path. Watch speed on return trip, as you can pick up speed to 15 mph quickly.
Conditions/Difficulty: Mostly dirt, cinder and gravel. Only one section of the trail still has railroad ties in place. Good ride for cross/hybrid bikes.
Points of Interest: River which runs along the park border in **Cedar Grove Park**. Watch for deer, rabbits and hawks.

This is a great beginner ride because it is straight and the grade is not really noticeable. It runs where there once was a railroad track. There is a nice stop at Cedar Grove Park, which has water fountains and restrooms during the summer months. The path is used by families and children, who might bring their dogs or "hot wheels". This trail is busiest after 5:30 p.m. during late spring, summer and early fall, so, please, ride with care!

There are three road crossings, two bridge crossings and on one of the bridges, the railroad ties are still in place. The ties can be ridden, but they are very bumpy. Beginners, please be cautious on this part of the path.

There is a hill at 0.4 miles which goes up and up for 0.2 miles, where you join the railroad path. Because most of the route follows the railroad, you should not get lost—trains didn't make turns!

Directions to Starting Point: From Interchange 53 off I-80, take Rt. 46 East to Browertown Rd. Turn right at the end of the ramp and follow to a "T". At the T, turn right onto Main Street. **Passaic Valley High School** is on the right (food is available at a store across the street from the high school).

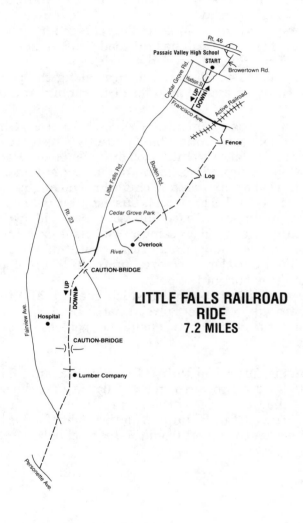

LITTLE FALLS RAILROAD
RIDE
7.2 MILES

PT.-PT.	CUME	DIRECTION	STREET/LANDMARK
0.0	0.0		From high school parking lot, bear right to **grassy clearing**. Ride to end of grassy clearing. Cross Hudson St. and climb up **sandy, gentle grade** (watch for deer toward the end)
0.4	0.4	**L**	Up steep hill on **Francisco Ave.** to second railroad track (first is active train track!)
0.2	0.6	**R**	Onto **dirt path**
0.1	0.7		Go around fence to the right of the high power electric wires overhead, but stay on the **main path**
0.3	1.0		Stay in the **center** and you will be above houses on the sides
0.3	1.3	**BL**	Stay on **main path** (two or three trails cut off to the right)
0.1	1.4		Go around log and ditch (beginners use side path on the left or walk bike)
0.1	1.5		Cross busy Bowden Rd. (*watch traffic!*). There are two possible paths to take. Stay to the **left** and follow **white arrow** which is painted on the road. Side trip: Go **straight** for 0.8 miles and look to where the railroad crosses the river. **Turn around**, come out and make a left and stay all the way to your right (side of opening). You will see the park just ahead — keep speed in check!
0.2	1.7	**SR**	Stay along side to the **far right**, the park is just over the small footbridge

PT.-PT.	CUME	DIRECTION	STREET/LANDMARK
0.0	1.7	**L**	Onto the **tar path**. You will be going off the tar path quickly and toward the baseball diamond. Path becomes obvious
0.2	1.9		There is a nice **view** of the river over the bridge
0.1	2.0	**SL**	Up the street towards the apartment complex. Watch for **white arrow** which points you toward the path. Enter the woods and come out on other side into driveway
0.1	2.1	**R**	**Path** is ahead. This is the section with the railroad ties still in place
0.0	2.1		Cross bridge over Rt. 23. *Beginners walk your bike over this part.* Once over the bridge, smooth sailing!
0.2	2.3		Gentle uphill — loose small stone path
0.1	2.4	**S**	On **main path**
0.1	2.5	**S**	Up gentle hill. Opening on right with road and open field (Essex County Psychiatric Hospital)
0.1	2.6		Cross bridge. *Walk bike across and watch your foot placement*
0.1	2.7	**S**	Go straight, but stay toward your right side (still gentle uphill)
0.2	2.9	**S**	Cross road. Lumber company on left. Path runs to right side of building
0.2	3.1	**S**	Cross Fairview Ave. (sign across street). Path picks up just to left side)
0.1	3.2		Re-enter woods
0.2	3.4		End of path. **Turn around** and head back
0.4	3.8	**S**	Cross Fairview Ave.

PT.-PT.	CUME	DIRECTION	STREET/LANDMARK
0.3	4.1	S	Cross road by lumber company (**Green Acres sign** shows path again)
0.1	4.2		Cross bridge. *This bridge comes up fast. Be careful and walk your bike*
0.2	4.4	**BR**	**Path** back into woods (hospital on left, small stones in path)
0.2	4.6	S	There is also a path on the right. Stay **straight** downhill!
0.3	4.9		Cross bridge. *Walk bike over railroad ties*
0.1	5.0	L	Once over bridge you come onto a driveway. Stay to the left. Sign on tree states **"path"**
0.0	5.0	L	Into woods, onto grass
0.0	5.0	R	Stay on right side and pick up road at apartment complex
0.1	5.1	R	**Over bridge** into park. Ride onto grass behind baseball cage. Go uphill to **tar path** by playground
0.2	5.3	R	Cross foot bridge, then ride up **grassy knoll.** Stay right to top
0.1	5.4	SL	Onto **path** again
0.3	5.7	S	Cross road. **Path** continues off slightly to the left by Green Acres sign, which is by curb opening
0.1	5.8		Go around tree and ditch. Stay to right
0.7	6.5	S	Go around fence to left. Continue on **path**
0.1	6.6	L	Stop at busy road (**Francisco Ave.**) and turn **left**. Do not cross to path on other side. Rather go downhill. *Watch your speed.* Cross active set of railroad tracks

PT.-PT.	CUME	DIRECTION	STREET/LANDMARK
0.2	6.8	**R**	Onto **path** by little brown house on right. Starts as tar
0.0	6.8	**S**	Slight downhill with small rocks and sand
0.4	7.2	**S**	Cross Hudson St. onto grass. Main St. is ahead of you, turn right to **high school**. End of route

PATRIOTS' PATH—5.6 OR 8.7 MILES

Terrain: Varied. Some sand, cinder and gravel packed dirt.

Conditions/Difficulty: Good conditions. Make sure you are proficient in the use of gears and brakes and have off-road tires. Hybrid bikes can be used, but a mountain bike is suggested. Both paths can be done in 2-4 hours.

Points of Interest: On the easy path, there is a river which runs on the right side on the return trip. This area contains many white-tail deer which are occasionally seen while riding on the path. The longer route's turn-around point is across the street from **Historic Speedwell Village**, where Alfred Vail and Samuel Morse tested the telegraph.

Patriots' Path is a longstanding greenway project of the Morris County Parks Commission and other agencies. It is designed to link major parks and areas of historical interest between the Morristown area and points east and west. The section of Patriots' Path covered by these routes are well-developed walking and mountain biking trails. They show the diversity of terrain and forest that make the Morristown area attractive.

Please note that bicycles are not allowed on the off-road trails of adjacent Jockey Hollow (Morristown National Historic Park).

Directions to Starting Point: The ride starts across from **Sunrise Lake, Lewis Morris Park**, between Morristown and Mendham. The parking area is on the right off westbound Rt. 24, four miles west of the Morristown Green.

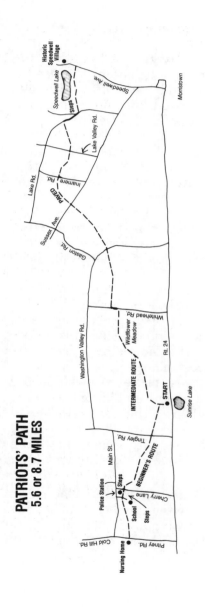

PATRIOTS' PATH
5.6 or 8.7 MILES

EASY ROUTE:

PT.-PT.	CUME	DIRECTION	STREET/LANDMARK
0.0	0.0	**L**	Exit parking lot and make a **left** before the bridge
0.3	0.3	**S**	Cross Tingley Rd.
0.6	0.9	**S**	Slight uphill
0.4	1.3	**S**	Follow **path** around and up (white fence on left)
0.1	1.4		*CAUTION! Steep short downhill with steps and a road (Cherry Lane) at the bottom.* Cross Cherry Lane and go **behind Mendham Township Police Station**, staying to your left past dog kennel. **Path** returns
0.1	1.5		**Path** continues (river on right)
0.0	1.5		Cross bridge over stream and go up steep incline with steps
0.0	1.5	**R**	**Path** continues to right at top of steps
0.1	1.6	**S**	Cross road near school. Walk bike down grade. Remount past foot bridge
0.8	2.4		**Turn around point**, opposite nursing home
0.8	3.2		Cross bridge, go uphill and cross road by school
0.2	3.4	**L**	Down short and steep hill with two bridges. *Stay to right to avoid steps. Lift front wheel onto bridge at bottom of hill*
0.8	4.2		Go **behind Mendham Township Police Station**. Stay to right in parking lot and cross street. You

PT.-PT.	CUME	DIRECTION	STREET/LANDMARK
			will see your next uphill once on top (nice view)
0.2	4.4		Downhill with fence on right, following **path**
0.3	4.7		Sandy downhill
0.3	5.0	**BR**	Onto gravel and follow the **path**
0.3	5.3	**S**	Cross Tingley Rd.
0.3	5.6	**R**	To **parking lot**; end of route

INTERMEDIATE ROUTE:

PT.-PT.	CUME	DIRECTION	STREET/LANDMARK
0.0	0.0	**S**	Cross bridge
0.1	0.1	**BR**	Follow **main path**
0.2	0.3	**R**	Go up hill with **main path**
0.3	0.6	**R**	Follow **dirt path**
0.2	0.8	**R**	Follow **dirt path**
0.3	1.1	**S**	Follow **white square markers** on trees
0.1	1.2	**L**	Onto **path**
0.1	1.3	**R**	**Path** continues
0.1	1.4	**L**	Pass first path. Take **second left** (by bench)
0.2	1.6	**L**	Downhill on **dirt path**. This turns into **gravel** once you leave forest and opens into a beautiful **wildflower meadow**
0.2	1.8	**S**	Cross Whitehead Rd. (actually turn **left** for 100 yards on road, and turn **right** to continue **path**)
0.5	2.3	**S**	Cross Washington Valley Rd. (loose stones)

PT.-PT.	CUME	DIRECTION	STREET/LANDMARK
0.7	3.0	S	Cross Sussex Ave. onto **paved path**
0.3	3.3	S	Cross Inamere Rd.
0.4	3.7	S	Cross Lake Valley Rd.
0.3	4.0	R	Onto **Lake Rd**. Pedal past recycling center and over bridge
0.5	4.5	L	Onto **Patriots' Path**. Stay to right side of path, as there are stairs
0.6	5.1		**Speedwell Lake** (swans, waterfall, **Historic Speedwell Village** across street). **Turn around**
0.2	5.3	BR	Onto **main path**
0.1	5.4		Uphill. Stay to left to miss stairs
0.0	5.4	R	At top of stairs onto **Lake Rd.**
0.1	5.5	BL	After crossing bridge, to continue on **Lake Rd.**
0.1	5.6	L	Onto paved **Patriots' Path**
0.5	6.1	S	Cross Lake Valley Rd.
0.4	6.5	S	Cross Inamere Rd.
0.3	6.8	S	Cross Sussex Ave. (loose stones and roots)
0.7	7.5	S	Cross Whitehead Rd., bearing gently to **left**. Enjoy view of **wildflower meadow**
0.3	7.8		Enter **forest** with slow uphill
0.1	7.9	R	Continue to follow uphill
0.1	8.0	R	Onto **path**. Watch for **white square markers** on trees
0.3	8.3	L	Onto **main path**
0.3	8.6	L	Onto **gravel path**
0.1	8.7	L	Over bridge to **parking lot**; end of route

RAMAPO MOUNTAIN STATE FOREST—7.1 MILES

Terrain: Long paved downhill road. Packed dirt, loose stones and a long winding uphill with a steady grade.

Conditions/Difficulty: Some sections have rocks the size of softballs which must be negotiated carefully. Since some log-jumping is required, a mountain bike would be best suited, although a cross-hybrid would suffice. There is also an active road, so one should be cautious of cars.

Points of Interest: There is a nice **vantage point** at the top which overlooks Ramapo Lake, the New York City skyline, and off to the west, the Wanaque Reservoir. At this point is the **ruins of an abandoned mansion**.

This is a beautiful ride for beginners. The path around the lake and the climb up to the lookout is well worth the effort.

The hill going back is quite an endurance climb. Off the lake are several trails. Some require more advanced skills, so be careful. One of these trails is known as the Cannonball, and is littered with rocks of various sizes. This trail has a red square marking.

Ringwood, in which Ramapo State Forest is located, was a large tract of land bought by Peter Hasenclever from David Ogden in 1764. The land included an iron furnace, several iron mines and a saw mill. This was the largest industrial business of the colonies.

The iron furnace built ammunition and cannons for the Continental Army. It also provided iron for the chain which hung in the Hudson River by West Point. The chain stretched 500 yards and stayed for five years.

A beginners' loop and an intermediate route are presented here.

Directions to Starting Point: Take I-287 to the Skyline Drive exit (a mile south of the connection with Rt. 208). Follow

Skyline Drive to the top, on the Ringwood/Oakland border, and park **across from Camp Tamarak** in a gravel parking lot.

BEGINNER'S LOOP *(described as narrative):*

From the parking area, go **around the fence** that closes off the road on the side of the lot. Exercise caution as this is an active roadway leading to a few private houses around Ramapo Lake.

In 0.5 miles, continue **straight** downhill past fire observation tower on right.

In another 0.6 miles, the **lake** will be straight ahead of you. A portable toilet is on the left.

Go **straight** over the **dam** and follow the path around the lake. From the dam it is 2.5 miles around. Beginners should **keep the lake on the right side** of your bicycle.

At the 2.3 mile point, turn **left** onto a road with two stone pillars with a chain laying off to the side. Take this road uphill for 1 mile.

In another 0.15 miles one encounters the **remains of a large mansion.** Ride or walk to the back of the ruins, lean the bike against the wall and walk down to the terrace to view New York City off to the left (east). The view west is of Wanaque Reservoir, and south one can see I-287.

After exploring the area of the ruins, **return down the hill** 1.1 miles and **bear left**. The lake will be visible from time to time on the right.

When you reach the dam, turn **left** and go up hill for 1 mile, watching for cars. Go past the ranger tower and stay to the right. The parking lot is at the top of the hill.

INTERMEDIATE ROUTE:

From the parking area, go **around the fence** that closes off the road on the side of the lot. Exercise caution as this is an active roadway leading to a few private houses around Ramapo Lake.

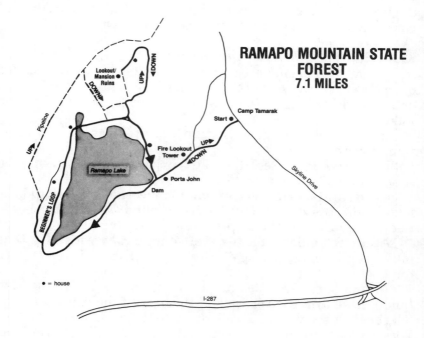

RAMAPO MOUNTAIN STATE FOREST
7.1 MILES

Lookout/
Mansion
Ruins

DOWN

UP

DOWN

Pipeline

UP

Camp Tamarak

Start

Fire Lookout
Tower

UP

DOWN

Ramapo Lake

BEGINNER'S LOOP

Porta John

Dam

Skyline Drive

● = house

I-287

PT.-PT.	CUME	DIRECTION	STREET/LANDMARK
0.5	0.5	S	**Downhill**, past fire observation tower on right
0.6	1.1		Porta John on left, lake straight ahead. **Cross dam**
1.0	2.1	L	Up and around in loose stones and gravel/sand
0.3	2.4	L	Around curve
0.1	2.5	R	**Uphill on pipeline**. Look to left for view!
0.6	3.1	R	On **fire road**. *Quick downhill, watch speed!*
0.3	3.4	L	Lake ahead
0.2	3.6	L	**Uphill**, great lookout at top. **Follow main road**, loose gravel/ stones
1.0	4.6	S	Past house
0.1	4.7	S	Up grassy road to **abandoned mansion.** Follow path straight around house. You will go over tile terrace to a staircase. *Proceed down with caution* (you can ride it if you are a strong intermediate). This is the **lookout**. Left is New York City, right is Wanaque Reservoir. After exploring area, go back on main trail. Use caution as people walk dogs and cars use it on occasion.
1.1	5.8	L	Onto **road which goes around lake**
0.2	6.0	L	By **dam** and Porta-John
0.6	6.6	R	Stay right by ranger house
0.5	7.1		Return to **parking lot**; end of route

SOUTH MOUNTAIN RESERVATION—2.8 MILES

Terrain: Rocky, root strewn. Good technical riding.
Conditions/Difficulties: This ride is for strong intermediates to advanced riders. Front suspension strongly recommended or the rider may come back beaten up and sore.
Points of Interest: 2048 acres of trails. Some nice rivers and a reservoir. Also Turtle Back Zoo is nearby.

Challenging **South Mountain Reservation** is a great area to ride and play in. There are many miles of carriage trails to ride; and there are areas that may become confusing. To avoid getting lost, bring a trail map of the reservation. This area is best travelled in groups for safety (use the buddy system).

The route described below is one of many trails available in the area. This ride takes approximately 1 to 1 1/2 hours. By following tree blazes one can ride for hours without taking the same trail twice. You can practice log hops and bunny jumping with the car still in view. Go out and enjoy!

Directions to Starting Point: Follow I-280 to Exit 7, "Pleasant Valley Way/Millburn". Turn left toward Millburn. Cross Northfield Ave. in about two miles, where Pleasant Valley Way changes name to Cherry Lane. Look for the **Tulip Springs parking lot** on the left, and park by the brick building.

PT.-PT.	CUME	DIRECTION	STREET/LANDMARK
0.0	0.0	S	Cross path across from brick building and climb up **short incline**
0.2	0.2	R	**Bear right** for next two forks
0.2	0.4	L	Stay on **main trail**
0.5	0.9	S	**Slight rocky uphill** (reservoir on left)
0.5	1.4		**Serpentine downhill**—watch the drainage ditch

PT.-PT.	CUME	DIRECTION	STREET/LANDMARK
0.5	1.9	**SL**	At back of Turtle Back Zoo. Pick up **tar road** and head **down embankment** into South Mountain Arena parking lot (restrooms are available in the arena). Go to main road (Northfield Ave.) onto **sidewalk** heading west into field
0.2	2.1	**L**	After going through field, onto **Cherry Lane**. Road ride begins
0.7	2.8	**L**	Into **Tulip Springs parking lot**. End of route

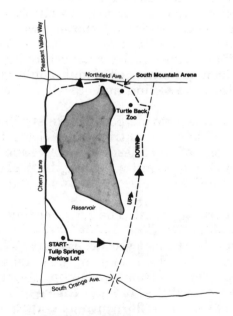

**SOUTH MOUNTAIN
RESERVATION**
2.8 MILES

SUSSEX BRANCH—11 or 16.4 MILES

Terrain: Gentle, rolling terrain; no steep hills. A great beginner's ride.
Conditions/Difficulty: Some sand, loose gravel and cinder on paths. Since this is an old railroad track, the route is straightforward with no sharp turns. Caution: There are a few bridge crossings.
Points of Interest: Many pretty meadows, a few lakes, lots of wildflowers and wildlife. Ride through an old railroad tunnel.

The Sussex Branch Trail, a unit of Swartswood State Park, is an abandoned railroad bed. For the most part, this railroad hugged present-day Route 206 as closely as a trolley line. This close access to the services of the highway makes it an excellent beginners' route.

The intermediate route, which starts further north, features more woods and fields as well as a section through Newton where one has to be a detective to find signs that a railroad once ran there.

Strong cyclists can combine both beginner and intermediate routes for a 27.4-mile round trip.

The northern end of the Sussex Branch connects with the Paulinskill Valley Trail, where very gung-ho cyclists can ride an additional 26.1 miles.

Directions to Starting Point: The beginner route starts near the **International Trade Zone** in Mt. Olive. Take I-80 West to Exit 25 (Rt. 206 North). At second light, turn left onto Rt. 604 West (Waterloo Rd.). In 1.8 miles, turn right into gravel parking lot (directly across from International Drive). The intermediate route starts at the "official" **Sussex Branch parking lot**. From I-80 West Exit 25, continue north on Rt. 206 5.7 miles past the second light (Waterloo Rd). Look for "Sussex Branch" sign on right. This is the parking lot for the trailhead.

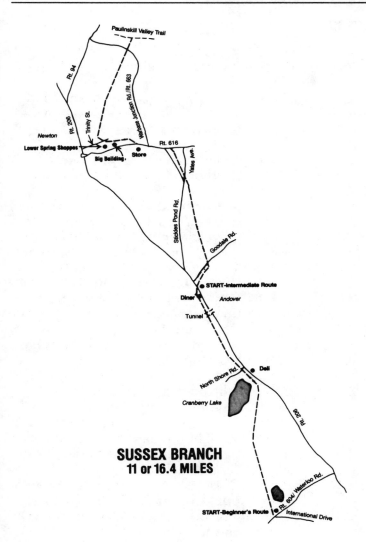

SUSSEX BRANCH
11 or 16.4 MILES

BEGINNER'S ROUTE

(Note: cue sheet describes only outbound route. Read up *for reverse-just like the old railroad timetables!)*

PT.-PT.	CUME	DIRECTION	STREET/LANDMARK
0.0	0.0	S	Go **around fence**
0.3	0.3		Pretty lake on right
1.5	1.8	S	Around fence to **right path**
0.1	1.9	**BR**	Road on left
0.1	2.0	S	Cross road. Path is straight ahead and **around two sets of fences** (lake off to left up slope). Stay on gravel, keeping lake on left
0.1	2.1	S	Fence, **stay to left** to get around
0.1	2.2	S	Through park and ride lot (big billboard). **Deli** across Rt. 206.
0.1	2.3	S	Cross North Shore Rd. and continue **straight**
0.5	2.8	L	Onto **side road** (path continues through woods, but is very rough)
0.3	3.1	R	**Up slope** back onto trail (ride in gully)
0.5	3.6	**BR**	Stay on **main trail**
0.1	3.7		*Caution: railroad tie bridge*
0.0	3.7	S	Go through big **tunnel**. Stay straight on main path
0.2	3.9	S	Cross High St. (grass path)
0.1	4.0	S	Cross Maple St.
0.1	4.1	S	Cross Brighton Ave. Go through **parking lot** (Railroad Ave. parallels on left and Andover Cycle is on the right)
0.2	4.3	S	By gravel lot at the end of the road. Pick up trail to left into woods

PT.-PT.	CUME	DIRECTION	STREET/LANDMARK
0.7	5.0	**S**	**Diner** down slope to right. Path narrows
0.1	5.1	**BR**	Ride through overgrown brush
0.2	5.3		You are by road (Rt. 206) with railroad tracks (non-active) in front of you
0.2	5.5	**L**	Cross Rt. 206. Trailhead on right by sign "Sussex Branch Trail". *Combined route cyclists, continue on the intermediate route.* Beginners, **U-turn**

INTERMEDIATE ROUTE:

(Note: cue sheet describes only outbound route. Read up *for reverse (just like the old railroad timetables!)*

0.0	0.0		Trail continues at end of gravel parking lot, past fence
0.3	0.3		View of lake on both sides
0.6	0.9	**S**	Cross road —**cinder path** ahead
1.7	2.6	**S**	Cross Yates Ave. (fence posts by trail)
0.4	3.0	**L**	You will come out of woods into town with sign stating "Welcome to Andover" on right. Turn **left** onto **Rt. 616 West**
0.5	3.5	**R**	Across from Quick Check, turn into **gravel lot**. Enter and take first trail on left going up the hill. Pass an electric substation on the right
0.2	3.7	**S**	Through parking lot by big empty building

PT.-PT.	CUME	DIRECTION	STREET/LANDMARK
0.3	4.0	S	Go **to right of "Lower Spring Shoppes"** into **gully** and continue
0.1	4.1	S	Cross Trinity St. into another **gully**
0.7	4.8	S	Very rocky riverbed, then trail opens up and smooths out
0.7	5.5	S	Through small river crossing
2.6	8.1	S	Cross Warbase Junction Rd./Rt. 663 (no sign)
0.1	8.2		**U-Turn** at junction of Paulinskill Valley Trail (sign says "Sussex Branch Lackawanna RR 1869-1953")

WE NEED YOUR HELP!

The information contained in this book was as accurate as could be determined at the time of publication. But roads change: housing developments spring up, towns decide to make through roads dead end, or new roads are built. And even occasionally, an error by a researcher, writer, author or publisher manages to make it to print.

That's why we at White Meadow Press rely on you, our readers, to help us keep our guidebooks up to date. If you see something on your bicycle that does not correspond to what's in this book, whether it be a cue sheet turn description, a line on a map, or text, please do not hesitate. When you get home from your ride, jot it down and send it off to us in a letter (be sure to pedal to the post office!). We will acknowledge your efforts with a return letter and a coupon good for one free book at your next purchase directly from the publisher.

Send your comments and notes to:

Anacus Press, Inc.
P.O. Box 4544
Warren, NJ 07059

ALSO:

If you enjoy writing and researching bicycle routes, we want to hear from you at the above address. We are always looking for new authors to expand our line of guidebooks, both local *RIDE GUIDE*s and our *Bed, Breakfast and Bike* series. Thanks!

ORDER THESE WHITE MEADOW PRESS BICYCLE GUIDES!

RIDE GUIDE/Central Jersey, by Dan Goldfischer ($9.95). Explore the horse country of Far Hills and Somerset County, the Princeton area, along the Delaware near New Hope and Lambertville, hilly Hunterdon County and the Jersey Shore from Sandy Hook to Island Beach.

RIDE GUIDE/Hudson Valley and Sound Shore, by Dan Goldfischer and Melissa Hefferman ($7.95). Features Westchester County, back-country Greenwich, views of Long Island Sound and the Greenwich Rivers, and the pretty (but hilly) Hudson Highlands by West Point and Bear Mountain.

Bed, Breakfast & Bike/New England, by Alex and Nancy May ($14.95). Come join the Mays as they visit 30 bike-friendly inns from Maine to Connecticut, and sample the best holiday bike riding in the region — as well as each inn's food and amenities! Two or more routes from each inn described in detail.

Bed, Breakfast & Bike/Mid Atlantic, by Alex and Nancy May ($14.95). The Mays take you from the Finger Lakes and Adirondacks of New York, through Pennsylvania's Amish Country and Bucks County, "down the shore" in New Jersey, Delaware, Maryland and Virginia and into the hills of West Virginia.

Bed, Breakfast & Bike/Northern California, by Naomi Bloom ($14.95). This big region on the West Coast contains every imaginable form of spectacular scenery, leading to some fantastic possibilities for country inn-based cycling. Thirty country inns are described from a cyclist's standpoint.

Bed, Breakfast & Bike/Pacific Northwest, by Carrie & Jon Muellner ($14.95). Mountains, seashore, farmlands and rain forest — the area from British Columbia to Oregon offers cyclists a little bit of everything. 32 bike-friendly inns are described.

Qty.	Please send me these books: Title	Amount
	Shipping	$2.00
	N.J. residents please add 6% sales tax	
	Total	

Send books to:

Name: _____

Address _____

City/State/Zip/Country: _____

Send coupon and payment to: Anacus Press, Inc., P. O. Box 4544, Warren, NJ 07059